# LOVE

## ON THE BRINK OF

# History

A Contemporary Ancient Spiritual Initiation

# Hannah Rappaport

For information, contact Nighthawk Press:
www.nighthawkpress.com

ISBN: 978-0615893334
Library of Congress Control Number: 2013951394

Cover artwork: The Antioch Chalice
Image copyright © The Metropolitan Museum of Art
Image source: Art Resource, New York

Portrait photograph of the author: Elida Hanson

Design: Lesley Cox, FEEL Design Associates, Taos, New Mexico
www.feeldesignassociates.com

Editing: Barbara L. Scott, Final Eyes, Taos, New Mexico
www.finaleyes.net

Jodie Barker, PhD

NIGHTHAWK PRESS
TAOS, NEW MEXICO

This book is dedicated to my daughter Sophia, my son Dickon, and my soul sister Kristine.

## I went and found my soul

I loved a man thought knightly fair
He took my love and bound it there
Where he did linger in the dark
With shrinking fear and
Sorrowed heart

A water king came rescued me
From shadows piercing ceaselessly
And I did love him soul-fully
He drank my love
Uncarefully

Alone unmet
In wilderness
A question mark upon my breast
Refined unknowing gives me rest
It is by life that I am blessed

∞

L'chaim

# Acknowledgments

Thank you to the people in this book. You each live in my heart in unique ways.

Thank you to the many writing coaches, teachers, and editors who have helped me over the years to bring this project to fruition.

Thank you to Barb Scott of Final Eyes, Rebecca Lenzini of Nighthawk Press, Lesley Cox of Feel Design Associates, and Jodie Barker, PhD, for your excellent support and skill in midwifing this project to completion.

I have the deepest gratitude for my parents, brother and sister, whose unconditional love is a profound source of stability for me.

I am ever grateful to Roger Weir and Nesa Weir whose penetrative seeing rockets beyond the bounds of this book.

I am deeply grateful for David Robinson's steadfast support through many painful changes, which has enabled me to pay forward the wisdom gathered.

# Table of Contents

# Preface

"We live not only our own life but the life of our time"

LAURENS VAN DER POST

We are living a time in History where women and men can no longer afford to be awkwardly running a three-legged race, joined at the hips to each other. Each soul must remember its mission and facility here on Earth for the sake of the soul of humanity. We no longer have the luxury to simply play personified roles such as wife or husband. This is not to say that women and men need be without each other. But we must learn to be together in new ways that don't hamper one another from fulfilling soul's purpose. History is calling us to remember the deeper aspects of our humanness. Without this reclamation we are trying to put together a thousand piece jigsaw puzzle with three-hundred pieces.

In the year 1991, an interior "voice" urgently prodded me, over and over: *Something has to be done.* According to Roger Weir, a private teacher of wisdom who sees humanity's plight spread out over very large time forms, 1991 was the end of an aeon — the pivotal turn of a two-thousand-year epoch.

Without comprehending the context, this reality pulled upon me to participate in it. I saw other women also hearing a clarion call that men were yet to attune to. Despite the valiant first attempts of the women's liberation movement, the encoding of our mothers' generation to "stand by your man" and be "the other half," "the woman behind the man" had strong roots, and many women defaulted to the programming of earlier generations. But the life that was upon us could no longer abide with old patterning and the old programs crashed, making mincemeat of many marriages.

My daughter attended a Waldorf school in which the children kept the same teacher from first to eighth grade. In 1985, when my daughter entered first grade, the parents of the class members were very involved. We met at swimming parties and volunteer events. It was a vibrant community of married couples, all supporting our children's education. That first grade class started out with thirty children each nestled within a traditional nuclear family. Eight years later, the same class with the same teacher had seen twenty-nine divorces, including the teacher's. We were all struggling to raise our children into a world we couldn't yet imagine, while we endured the dismantling of old paradigms.

This account is about how I attempted to make sense of the chaotic historical wave that was, and is more so now, upon us all at the outset of a new aeon.

Spurred by a soul urge to take possession of my true name, I wanted to make a ceremony of my name change and chose to be baptized at the Ecclesia Gnostica, by Stephan Hoeller, the Hungarian Gnostic bishop whose church was housed in a storefront on Hollywood Boulevard in California. I had attended services and lectures there for several years, and Stephan had become a friend.

What I have called "that dinky little ceremony" set in motion seven years of mystical experiences: dreams, visions, and synchronicities. I was sucked from present time into "presence" — a timeless dimension where ancient myths and mysteries are not past and dead but quite alive and very real, leading to the revelation that history is not dry dates long gone, frozen on dusty pages, but a dimension of human endeavor, ever presently marking our place in the cosmos.

There are increasing volumes of scholarship about Gnosticism and early Christianity. What follows is not a scholarly work but my attempt to communicate the very personal life transformation that ensued from that baptism.

May the blessings that unfold from my experiences cast their light upon whomever finds this book.

HANNAH RAPPAPORT ∞ TAOS, NEW MEXICO ∞ 2013

# The Sacred Call
# Comes from Nothing

---

"With tears that cleanse the spirit and carry it away
to the burning lemon grove of love."

FEDERICO GARCÍA LORCA

---

# The Wild Vanquished Feminine Beckons

I am about five years old, playing with the kids in one of the backyards across the street from my home in a suburban Los Angeles tract-house neighborhood. I need to go home and pee. Our door is locked. I knock and bang on the door, crying out, "Mommy," but she isn't there. I can't get into the house and I pee in my pants. Ashamed, not wanting to go back and play with the other kids, I tumble into a deep loneliness. I want my mommy. As the pee seeps down the legs of my pants, a deepening sorrow seeps into my heart, which balloons out of proportion to my current predicament.

I crumple on the front lawn, curling my knees to my chest, face in the grass. I duck and cover as they told us to do at school, under the desks, to practice for the atom bomb that we are told could drop on us, to rehearse for when we see that ominous mushroom cloud silently rise from the earth, to prepare for seeing the bones through our flesh. My face presses into the grass; the itchy imprint of dry prickly crab grass blended with the smooth, moist, rounded *Dichondra* grass, which my mother works tirelessly to cultivate every morning by pulling weeds when the ground is still dewy from the night before. Tears of mourning drench my face. I no longer feel childish shame over peeing in my pants but the shame of humanity for all that is fallen from the Garden of Eden, from the kingdom of heaven, from the heart of mankind. I cry and my tears are a release, a cleansing comfort. There is luxury in my tears and in the darkness of the earth that holds me – the ground, the grass, the smell of soil and green, the colony of ants venturing over the territory of my fingers. There is comfort and goodness in my tears and in my solitary sorrow embraced by all the sorrow that ever was.

Suddenly I hear a kind voice and then feel a hand on my shoulder trying to lift me, to console me. It is Alicia, the dancer, the nice neighbor with the long strawberry-blond hair who sometimes gives my older brother and me a dime to help her make the beds or rake the leaves. She wants to comfort me, not knowing my tears are my comfort. "Your mommy has just gone to the market. She'll be back very soon," she says.

"Leave me alone," I cry, not wanting to be disturbed from my communion with sorrow. I pull myself from her. I am desperate to return to the magic I tasted in the dark underworld of dirt and grass – a union of tears and heaven. Some interior mystery is unfolding; there is something profoundly feminine in that darkness that holds deeper sway than Alicia's sincere compassionate offer to help bring me back into the daylight. How deeply has the feminine been submerged that she must call me, at such a young age, to these depths? Alicia leaves me alone, but the spell is broken. Soon my mother returns, takes me into the house, changes my pants, and makes me a peanut-butter-and-jelly sandwich on white bread, placed on an orange plastic plate with a plastic cup of milk that she tricks me into drinking because the peanut butter is so sticky in my mouth.

# Like Jesus

My little red sandals protect my soles from burning as I walk on the hot summer sidewalk, yet my soul burns with a huge question: *How should I live this life?* As if I turned over an old silver dollar from tails to heads, the answer is revealed in my mind, born from a consciousness older and wiser than my seven years: *Try to live as much like Jesus Christ as you can.*

I was not raised in a Christian tradition. There is a Star of David in my aura. I was born in Israel in 1951, three years after it was declared a country. Though my family is strongly identified with being Jewish, they returned to the U.S.A. from Israel when I was six months old. I'd never heard the name Jesus from my parents or in our home. I knew nothing of the mythologies of Christianity: the man on the cross, the death and resurrection, the twelve Apostles, or the virgin mother. Yet this visionary guidance to *try to live like Jesus Christ* did not seem strange to me; it felt completely natural and right. I had an intuitive sense that Jesus Christ was a Man of Light, a human being of a higher order. My spirit knew Jesus as a highly evolved eternal "Person" who was not trapped in delusions, one who living by love was freed even from death.

I didn't feel the need to talk to anyone about my vision. I didn't feel guilty for the love I felt for Jesus Christ. This love belongs to the world inside me that is self-sustaining. This experience caused me to feel very different from the world around me. I was being guided from within by an eternal part of my being to reach for that higher order. Whatever my mitochondrial DNA inheritance, my spirit inheritance came from this other dimension.

I did not begin to remember this until I was forty years old.

# CHAPTER I

# Baptism

---

"And they made a compact with me,
and wrote it in my heart, that it might not be forgotten"

HYMN OF THE PEARL

---

*"Will the candidate for baptism please step forward."* The bishop's voice is more like talk than the hypnotic rhythm that rolls through his Hungarian accent during the regular parts of the Gnostic Mass. I step forward to the rickety portable kneeling rail. Two priests flank the bishop: the Norwegian figurative painter Jan Saether and John Goelz, affectionately known as Jack-the-Bear.

Jan (pronounced "Yon") looks into my eyes with penetrating blue saucers, two oceans that sparkle with the diamonds of sunrise. John Goelz's lips turn upward, a hearty bowl of kindness, with a glint of irony in his eyes. They both stand four inches taller than Stephan Hoeller, the bishop, who places his hands, strong and gentle, over my head as he incants some prayers. The three of them are decked out in frayed and fading High Church raiment.

I bow my head over a cheap shell-shaped silver bowl. Droplets fall close before my eyes as the bishop dribbles consecrated holy water onto my head three times. *"I baptize thee Hannah Ethel, in the Name of the Father, and of the Son, and of the Holy Spirit."*

Stephan affectionately pats my hair dry with a white folded linen. I lift my head to a waft of fragrant smoke coming from the censer in Jan's hands. The bishop hands me a candle, which he has lighted from the row of candles burning in their polished brass holders on the altar behind him. His large amethyst ring glints before my eyes as he places the white cotton scarf I've brought for the ritual over my shoulders. It is February 3, 1991. I am forty years old and finally taking possession of my true name, *Hannah*.

After the ceremony, a pair of pastel blue freestanding screens is placed in front of the altar. One of the clerics sets up a card table with cheap wine and store-bought cookies. Congregants come up to congratulate me on my baptism and new name. I feel like exposed photo paper, immersed in the chemical solution that will now turn the plain white sheet into an image.

Jan Saether comes through the white satin curtains from behind the sanctuary, still vested in his shabby white chasuble. He stands at the seam where gold carpet meets brown, marking the line between sanctuary and nave, where the congregation sits. His strong musk is mixed with the faint scent of turpentine and incense. In a low, resonant Norwegian accent he says, "They couldn't see you, but I saw you, and you looked very beautiful." I look into his unflinching eyes, bluer than any powder blue I can remember, though standing here facing him I have the strange sense of remembering…

# Wandering in the Desert

I hated school from the start. Compared to the other world of which I was a part, it felt deeply and painfully irrelevant.

In second grade, I had a dream: I am walking to school in the early morning, completely alone. I arrive through the gate of the chain-link fence that encloses the playground, a flat two acres of black tarmac with white lines of paint that designate the games we are allowed to play: sock ball, tether ball, handball. In the dream, the playground is completely fogged in; blinded by a mist, I am unable to find my way toward familiar landmarks.

One morning as I walked to school with my older brother Gideon, the foggy playground of my dream occurred in waking life.

Both the dream and waking experience of being in a fog characterize my memory of childhood. The most distinctive feelings I recall are those of having terrible stomachaches. I have always had stomachaches. Perhaps these two sensations – one of being totally undefined and the other that, when I was defined, I was in pain – caused me to feel like an outsider. Other kids seemed perfectly happy playing ball games. They seemed to know how things were done, while I felt somewhat disembodied – when I wasn't in pain. Wanting to be like Jesus in a Jewish family did not help me feel connected to my environment.

My second-grade class let out twenty minutes earlier than Gideon's class. I would wait for him after school so we could walk home together. I recall waiting at the gate, examining my dirty fingers hooked around the chain-link fence, the smell of acrid metal and playground dust permeating my nostrils. I count my fingers, representing the grades I'll have to go through before I don't have to go to school anymore: third, fourth, fifth, up to twelfth grade. Each finger represents a year of waiting to be free to explore my inner world – unrestricted by the boundary lines that corral play, free from the loud, harsh buzzers that designate time slots – where silence is given space.

That was when I took my first vow. It was the kind of vow that ends up being kept even when you've forgotten you made it. I vowed that as soon as I was not obliged to go to school, I wouldn't. I had a sense that college was optional and I would not exercise my option. Going along with institutionalized learning did not support my inner vision of being like Jesus.

∞

At the age of fourteen, I told my mother I wanted to be sixteen for the rest of my life. In Los Angeles, where the automobile was your ticket to ride and sixteen was when you could get a driver's license, sixteen meant freedom. Wanting to be like Jesus had faded into the background of my consciousness...

"But already the man has begun to realize the freedom
of the cosmos; he has begun to feel himself a true cosmopolitan
or world-citizen, and to thrill in harmony with the Powers.
He experiences an ineffable union that removes all fear,
and longs for the consummation of the final Sacred Marriage
when he will perform the great sacrifice,
and of himself make joyful surrender of all that he has been
in separation, to become, by union with Those alone
who truly are, all that has ever been and is and will be
—and so one with God, the All and One."

HYMNS OF HERMES, BY G.R.S. MEAD

As an adult, my brother once told me, "When you were three years old and they said you couldn't cross the street, you just didn't believe them." By age sixteen I didn't want to believe in limitations. The hippie "free love" counterculture was in full swing. I passed my driver's test on the first try and was allowed to borrow the family car from time to time. My best friend Sandee, however, had her *own* car.

Sandee and I met in eleventh grade while standing in line at the work/study counselor's office to have our papers stamped. We were both enrolled in a program that kept us in school for only half a day. After lunch we would go to our paying jobs.

I inherited tailoring talents from my maternal grandparents. I knew them well growing up, since they, too, lived in Los Angeles. They were both Polish/Hungarian immigrants. My grandfather had studied history and wanted to be a teacher but ended up working in a suit factory. My grandmother was a trained dress designer who could whip up any fashionable dress she saw hanging on a mannequin in a store window.

For my work/study program I was employed at a clothing store in West Hollywood: The Great American Clothing Experiment. It was one of the first "unisex" jeans and t-shirt stores in Los Angeles, on the corner of Santa Monica Boulevard and Doheny Drive. I worked upstairs from the shop, sewing African shirts of imported African printed fabrics. Sandee worked at a dry cleaner.

On weekend nights, Sandee and I would take "uppers," drive to Sunset Strip in her yellow Volkswagen Beetle, and meet up with friends while we checked out the hippies and rockers. We'd park the car and walk around socializing with the colorful crowd, the scents of patchouli and marijuana mixing with charbroiled hamburgers from the sidewalk patio of Hamburger Hamlet. When we were really wired, we'd drive up Laurel Canyon into the hills and slowly weave our way through the side streets, past houses built on stilts and shrouded in bougainvillea or framed by banana fronds. Rolling across Mulholland Drive at twenty miles an hour, with the sparkling lights of the valley below, I felt the sense of freedom I wanted my life to exemplify.

In our sixteen-year-old pumped-up minds we were having profound philosophical conversations. One recurring discussion centered on love. Sandee contended, "The truck driver who is out on the road listening to country music, popping uppers for weeks at a time, then comes home to his honey, slaps her around a bit before they have mad passionate sex – that's love."

"That's not love," I'd counter. "I don't know what that is, but it's not love. Love is something spiritual, not just attachment."

I was raised on solid, unerring, unconditional love. My parents were my template for loving and being loved by God; but at sixteen, I didn't dare tell them about our forays to Sunset Strip, smoking pot, taking uppers and driving around.

# Discovering the Gnostic Church

"Everyone you meet is an angel with a message for you.
It's your job to discern what that message is."

BISHOP STEPHAN HOELLER

By age twenty-four I was married to David, an Englishman. He was both a songwriter and a lawyer, and for me a divine messenger, facilitator of the light I'd always longed for.

David and I arrived at a Hollywood Hills party where a picture window framed the Hollywood sign. It was the late-1970s. Our hostess was in the corner of the dining area speaking French to an older man. I waved to my old friend King, who was strumming his acoustic guitar near a table littered with open wine bottles. David and I sat side by side on a down sofa; he reached for a large book displayed on the coffee table. It was cloth covered and expensive looking. We read the title by the orange glow from a Tiffany lamp: *The Secret Teachings of All Ages,* by Manly P. Hall. He lifted the book onto his lap and opened it at random to a page with gilded words, "I felt strongly moved to explore the problems of humanity, its origin and destiny." David turned to the table of contents, where together we saw titles like, *The Life and Writings of Thoth Hermes Trismegistus; Qabbalistic Keys to the Creation of Man; The Theory and Practice of Alchemy; Mystic Christianity.* The book contained beautiful color images full of symbolism and mystery.

Our hostess migrated over to us and sat on the coffee table facing us. "You've found one of my most precious possessions."

"Where did this come from?" David asked. He did not take his eyes from the pages as he turned them slowly, drinking in images of winged horses and archangels.

"I got it from PRS, The Philosophical Research Society, just over on Los Feliz Boulevard, near the entrance to Griffith Park. It's a place the author founded, back in the early 1930s. Yeah, Manly Hall dedicated his life to the study of religion, mythology, metaphysics, the occult, that sort of thing. He's got a huge library there."

As an avid reader, hearing "huge library" was enough for David. The following afternoon while I was at work, he browsed the bookstore of The Philosophical Research Society. He noticed a flyer posted on the bulletin board:

*The Gnostic Society.*
*Lectures Every Friday Night:*
*Jung and Gnosis, Alchemy and Gnosis,*
*The Major Arcana of the Tarot.*

David had studied comparative religion in England and knew about the Gnostics – early mystical Christians who had been rejected and persecuted by the canonical church as heretics. He found his way to the address on the flyer.

The Gnostic Society was housed in a storefront at the intersection of Hollywood Boulevard and Sunset Boulevard. You could have walked past the picture framer and the antique junk store on either side of it and never noticed it unless you were interested in that which is esoteric and occult, because the windows were paneled over and painted white. To see the small announcement window set discretely in the door with the schedule of events, you would have had to be drawn up close by some magnetic curiosity.

That night, David, King, and I were sitting in Canter's Deli after midnight when David told the story of his first encounter with the Gnostic Society. The waitress had just left the table with our order.

"There was a strong smell of burnt incense as I entered the dowdy room, with worn brown carpet. Shadows were cast by folding chairs set in rows from a lamp in the corner. Two freestanding wood screens stood behind a large wooden armchair – like a throne, with a red velvet seat cushion. I half expected the ghost of Jean Harlow to toss over a red satin robe from behind one of those powder-blue screens," David chuckled.

"I heard water running from somewhere in the back, and just as I was examining a large quilted image of a snake curled into a circle, eating its own tail, the faucet handle squealed and the water stopped running.

"From behind, I heard, 'May I help you?'" David said he turned to see a small, roundish man emerge from behind some white satin curtains. The curious figure sported a goatee with no mustache, his thinning hair home-dyed brown. He was dressed in a slightly worn dark wool suit with a red silk cravat. He held a sponge in one hand and a bottle of household cleaner in the other.

"His dark eyes kept shifting between me and the front door," David told us as we all dove our spoons into matzo-ball soup, "and he kept bowing at the waist."

David had an uncanny ability to identify a person's nationality. "I recognized his Hungarian accent immediately. He was Old World dignified, and I felt transported back in time to nineteenth-century Budapest."

"I'm interested in the lecture," David had said, smiling hopefully at the goateed Hungarian man with uneven eyebrows.

"Yes, you are welcome, but the lecture doesn't begin until seven. I'm just preparing."

Building the suspense, David told us, "He shifted his eyes again toward the door and then said to me, 'Tell me, how did you come in?'"

"I didn't understand what he was asking." David paused his story for effect.

"I'm just wondering how you got in," the man repeated.

"I don't understand," David said to him, still uncertain what he wanted to know. "I opened the door and came in."

"But the door was locked. I'm sure I locked it when I arrived. I always lock it while I'm preparing for the lecture."

I imagine they both chuckled nervously. "Well, I'll go get something to eat and be back at seven then." David was always able to rely on British formality.

"Yes, I will enjoy having you. I am Bishop Stephan Hoeller. I'm the lecturer and, as you can see, also the janitor of this establishment." He was still holding the sponge and spray bottle.

Magical things like opening locked doors were not foreign to either man. Later, when we got to know Stephan, he would tell stories about the ghosts of his childhood Hungarian estate. David's mother used to say, "Oh, we're all a bit like that," in her formal British accent, when speaking of psychic occurrences.

David continued to attend the Friday-night lectures, and when I was not working I joined him.

# First Mass

In February of 1979, I was three months pregnant with Sophia, our first child. After having attended several of Dr. Hoeller's Friday-night lectures, David and I decided to check out the Sunday morning Gnostic Mass. Ecclesia Gnostica was the church component of the Gnostic Society, housed in the same storefront, at the crossroads of Hollywood and Sunset boulevards.

About twenty people were scattered throughout the seats, some together, most sitting singly, apart. Two long-haired young men in dirty jeans with chains and tattoos sat in the front row, quiet, meditative. A tall, white-haired, elegantly dressed woman sat alone. A neatly dressed elderly couple walked in and sat quietly. David and I settled onto the uncomfortable folding chairs. The "Jean Harlow" screens had been removed, revealing a heavy wooden altar covered by starched white linens. Six brass candlesticks were lined up in sets of three at the front of the altar, flanking a brass cross that was planted into a wooden plinth painted gold. The cross did not have a tortured body hanging from it; rather, three bulbs blossomed from each of the extensions. Other ritual implements, foreign to me, gave weight and authority to the rundown room with cracked plaster walls. A few men and women moved in and around the altar, arranging one thing or another, silently, reverently, preparing for the Mass, then disappeared to a back room behind white satin curtains.

All of these Christian symbols fascinated me. I grew up in a world where one was either Jewish or not Jewish. All forms of Christianity were the same to me – not Jewish – and I simply had no experience of them. My "eternal moment" as a child, of wanting to be like Jesus Christ, had nothing to do with the formal and political religions that fall under the umbrella of Christianity; that had come from a higher order of consciousness.

Stillness among the congregants had settled in, and a bell tinkled from behind the curtains. A group of satin-vested men and women came out around the altar, with Stephan at the center. I recognized some of them from the lectures.

It requires a suspension of disbelief to take seriously a High Church ritual performed in a storefront on Hollywood Boulevard. David and I had to quickly avert each other's glances and turn our attention back to the altar to keep from chuckling.

Stephan recites passages from a book, and people move in smooth choreography around the altar. Some time into the performance, he removes a white cloth from the center, uncovering a gold chalice. I become so lightheaded I think, *I am about to faint.* I fold myself over. *Isn't that what you're supposed to do when you feel faint, put your head between your legs?* I've never fainted before. I've also never experienced anything so "mystical" during a religious service before. Something "other" seems to be taking place that I cannot explain or understand. But without a doubt, I feel it. There is a deep resonance with that inner part of me that I have almost forgotten –

that part of me that was told to *try to live as much like Jesus Christ and I can.*

I learned later that this uncovering of the chalice is the beginning of the consecration – the part of the rite where the Christ is invited to be present in the wine and bread.

After the Mass, the bishop, divested of his ritual garments, came up to me with a glass of water. He'd noticed me putting my head down. "It was probably just all the incense smoke," he said. "And in your condition." But though his words were dismissive, his dark eyes fixed upon mine as if he were trying to remember where we'd met before, even though we'd already become well acquainted during the several times I'd been to his lectures.

∞

On February 6, 1990, one year before my baptism, I had a life-altering dream: I awake from sleep (in the dream), get up, and go to the little bathroom en suite to our bedroom. Perched on the faucet is a large eagle. I am very impressed by its talons, which are curved over the handles of the tap. Slowly and carefully I turn the handles to run the water. As an offering of respect, I dribble water onto the bird's talons. I am anointing it. The eagle is very stern, yet I don't feel threatened, but rather reverential.

When I actually awoke from the dream I felt that something momentous had occurred. My waking state felt more like sleep than the awakening in the dream.

Shortly after that dream, I began reading *The Hymn of the Pearl*, an ancient Gnostic allegory of the soul's purpose on Earth. I sat in amazement, recognizing the same symbolic elements as in my dream, as I read the following passage:

And serving as messenger
the letter was a letter
sealed by the king with his right hand
against the evil ones, the children of Babel
and the savage demons of Sarbug.
It rose up in the form of an eagle,
the king of all winged fowl;
it flew and alighted beside me,
and became speech.
At its voice and the sound of its rustling
I awoke and rose from my sleep.
I took it, kissed it,
broke its seal and read.
And the words written on my heart
were in the letter for me to read.
I remembered that I was a son of kings
and my free soul longed for its own kind.
I remembered the pearl
for which I was sent down into Egypt.

HYMN OF THE PEARL

# My True Name

Why did my parents name me Ethel? My paternal grandfather insisted that I take the name of his deceased wife, my father's mother, whom Saba (grandfather in Hebrew) adored, even after he had remarried. It is Jewish custom to name a baby after someone who has died. This was a convention Saba desired to uphold, I believe more for the sake of keeping his beloved alive than for the custom itself. I suppose my parents didn't think they had any other choice –

they were not rebellious types – unlike Saba, who was considered a heretic at the yeshiva in Russia when he was a boy because he secretly read Tolstoy, Dostoyevsky, and other Russian authors forbidden by the orthodoxy.

Saba was one of the founders of the State of Israel – a Socialist, a Zionist, a pioneer; he was not a fundamentalist worshiper. Ethel, his wife, was his consort in those ideals and adventures. I felt a deep connection with my grandfather – not with his idealism about Israel, but with his spirit, with his courage to reach beyond religious conventions.

My father never spoke much about his mother when I was growing up. But one day when I was about thirty-five and with a little daughter of my own, my father said, "I don't think you know this, but my mother's first name was Hannah. She preferred going by her middle name, Ethel." He did not realize he had just given me *my* true name.

My father has a way of *knowing things.* Things just come to his mind. Watching him do a crossword puzzle is fascinating. He sits down with his coffee, spreads out the morning paper's crossword page, then simply writes the words in, one after another. He doesn't stop to think. I have the impression that he sees the answers hanging like word fruit in mid air, ripe for plucking, to place onto the page. I'm sure the thought to tell me that my grandmother's first name was Hannah came to him like that, instantly, from spirit.

∞

As my fortieth birthday approached, I began to feel my soul stirring. A few years earlier, David and I had taken a trip to Israel with Sophia, who was five at the time, to visit my ninety-four-year-old Saba. He told me about some of his dreams: "In my dreams I am always in my forties."

I've studied my dreams extensively and read C.G. Jung, Joseph Campbell, and other scholars of symbology for many years. I no longer "interpret" dreams. I recognize dreams as direct experience. If a ninety-four-year-old man is still forty in his dreams, that age must be a relevant peak in the course of a life. My mother, fond of aphorisms, always said, "Life begins at forty." If my life was about to begin, I wanted it to be with my real name.

I decided to take possession of my true name. The name Hannah is actually on my Israeli birth certificate, as my middle name, but it is in Hebrew, which I cannot read. Somehow, on the sea voyage that brought my family back to the United States from Israel when I was an infant, I became a child made of shorthand. The Palindrome H's were dropped, and my middle name became Anne. But I could not know myself by the name I was called. Ethel was always a problem in my mouth. My tongue got tangled by "TH" and locked in by "L." Ethel was a noble name in my parents' time – Ethel Merman, Ethel Barrymore – but in my time it meant gasoline: high-octane Ethyl. The boys in school would tease, "Let's go down to the gas station and pump Ethel."

I was encouraged to make the change by my British mother-in-law. She was known by her middle name, Sheila. And Sheila was a force to be reckoned with, the archetypal British "she-who-must-be-obeyed." One afternoon while she and my father-in-law were visiting us from England, sitting on the patio drinking tea, I mentioned that I wanted to start using Hannah. Other people had thought it would be difficult to get friends and family to change. But stout Sheila sat there at the patio table, arms crossed over her ample breasts, and said, "you just *make* them call you what you want them to call you." And that was that.

On a Sunday morning, about a month before my fortieth birthday, I attended the Gnostic Mass. By that time David and I were living in suburbia, the San Fernando Valley, and his Sunday sacrament was football. After Mass, I approached Stephan, the bishop, and asked, "Is there some kind of a name-changing ceremony?" The congregation of the tattered little storefront church had migrated to where a jug of cheap Chablis was being poured. The brass censer still exuded fragrance through diamond-shaped holes. The bishop's dark jaunty eyes sparkled under those uneven eyebrows, "You haven't been baptized yet..."

*Why not, I trust him.* I had no comprehension then of how heavily I would come to rely on that trust, or how deeply it would influence the course of my life.

∞

In Judaism there is a ritual called the mikvah, which is an immersion in water for the sake of purification. The ritual traditionally involves many rules and subtleties, but in essence I believe it is the root source of the Christian ritual of baptism. I knew then and still know very little about the mikvah. For me the external accouterments of ritual forms mean less than their essence. I was to be purified for the sake of my authentic name. Call that Jewish, Christian, Gnostic... I doubt the trappings matter much to God.

## Commitment to Compromise

Two weeks after my baptism, David and I celebrate my fortieth birthday by staying in a quaint bed & breakfast north of the Golden Gate Bridge. After a wine-soaked, candlelit dinner in the city, I wake in the middle of the night, slip out from under the hand-stitched patchwork quilt and pad across the room to the bathroom, my feet pressing against cold tiles. I shiver in the chilly bathroom, then return to the warm bed next to my husband of almost fifteen years. I feel comfortable and cozy with his familiarity. We have been through our marital challenges: illness, betrayal, neglect, disillusionment, as well as shared joy, romance, good sex, children, and belonging.

Though our domestic relationship has, for me, become a compromise to my soul's longing for spiritual freedom, for the love of a fully realized life, I feel at this moment – *I can make this compromise.* There will be more challenges, but there will be weddings and funerals and family visits, and perhaps grandchildren. And I will find comfort in these things. *I can do this. I can stay married. I can continue to be "a wife."*

I settle into resignation under the quilts in the chilly room. My childhood vision of wanting to live as much like Jesus Christ as I can is eclipsed by this convention – marriage. *Isn't marriage, after all, the right and safe circumstance for a woman?*

I rest into forgetfulness, into staying with what I know, into this domestic circle that portrays itself as safety. This will be good enough for a life. *I can do this.* I snuggle closer to the warm body sleeping next to me and fall back to sleep.

∞

I don't claim greatness at anything, but I was soon reminded that committing to compromise was not written in the book of my life. Through the events that followed, my spirit shouted: *What? You've got to be kidding!*

# CHAPTER 2

# Confirmation

# Archetypal Women

As a married woman, like my mother, my emotional fealty had been with my husband. I had projected my innate love of God onto him, and he received it willingly. As my interior remembering grew stronger, a subtle competition between my husband and my divine longing emerged – a kind of jealousy he had of God. I had no girlfriend confidants during my marriage and no emotional bonds outside my family.

I began to feel part of a larger community with the Gnostic Ecclesia. Roberta, who most people called Bobbie, was Bishop Stephan's "wife." If there had ever been an official ceremony consecrating their "marriage" it probably had been a very private thing. Regardless, Bobbie was a true consort and was dedicated to Stephan and his work. Her sister, Laurel, was very close to both Bobbie and Stephan, and the three of them were often together.

Bobbie and Laurel were both beautiful and reserved women. Their father had been an international businessman, and they had been raised in Japan. The sisters were of Jewish descent and carried themselves with what I've come to call a "Jewess" quality. When it has not regressed into arrogance and self-entitlement, this quality stands as testimony to a deep taproot in grace, humility, and compassion. With the Japanese modesty as an overlay, they were both deeply feminine assets to Stephan and his church.

Often when I'd arrive at church before Mass, Bobbie and Laurel would fawn over my clothes. If I'd come in after the congregation had quieted to internal dimensions, their eyes would grow large, and they'd smile their gracious smiles, nodding approval and touching their own skirts or sleeves to indicate they liked my look. I began to make a special effort when dressing for church. David liked to buy me clothes, and I had several Laise Adzer designer garments, Middle Eastern–inspired draped rayon skirts and shawls that I mixed and matched with various accessories. These were favorites of Bobbie and Laurel.

# Feminine Innocence

One Sunday before my baptism, when David was still coming with me to church, a slender well-dressed woman in a classic straight camel-colored skirt, silk blouse, and a string of real pearls round her neck, sat down next to me. "I'm Kristine," she smiled sweetly. We'd seen each other a few times before but had not spoken. She told me she was an artist. "I paint and work in the clay," she said. I had also embraced pottery as my artistic expression. I hadn't abandoned clothing design, the vocation I'd inherited from my maternal grandparents, but after my daughter was born I needed something more.

Kristine and I talked about our art. "I have a kiln and glaze studio in the barn at my home in the valley," I said. We talked about getting together to make art in my studio. I later learned that seeing me at church with my children and David, Kristine had the impression that I had the glorious idyllic life of a happy creative woman: "The white picket fence, the rose garden, happy children playing in the yard while you make your art, your husband totally supportive in every way, cradled in the bosom of your family."

Kristine has told me this story many times. "And then you told me your name was Ethel and it was like, everything just broke. Like in a fairy tale when she's fed a poison apple, or her hands are cut off. The deal is made with the devil, the leaves fall off the trees, the season changes. All of that happened like that," she snapped her fingers, "in that moment when you said your name. It was like you were under a spell. And I really didn't see you until you started to emerge from all of those things that weren't you, including your name." Kristine's perception works with a unique accuracy, like mythology itself, seeing the composition of a circumstance in its wholeness, not fragmented. That day when we first spoke, Kristine tore off a bank deposit slip to give me her phone number.

"I was always making friend deposits," she giggled.

I hadn't had a close girlfriend since Sandee. After Sandee and I were both married, our lives diverged. I became swallowed up in my marriage and interested in the threads of knowledge that David and I were pursuing: mythology, psychology, symbolism, Gnosticism. Sandee had followed a more pragmatic life: raising her children and tending to the needs of her home and husband.

Kristine possessed an innate feminine Earth-magic sensibility, like the Pagans of her Irish ancestry. She came to the Gnostic church by means of her art. She was a friend of the Norwegian priest, Jan Saether and his ex-wife Liv, who was a deacon in the Gnostic clergy. Jan and Liv Saether cofounded an art school in West Los Angeles called Bruchion. Though their marriage had ended, they were still friends and partners at the school, each teaching their own classes. They shared parenting their son, and participated together in the Gnostic Eucharist.

Jan was a figurative art teacher, and Kristine came to him to learn; but actually she just painted in his studio. He once said she was the only artist he wouldn't dare try to teach. "She has her own instinctive wisdom about her images – sexual and innocent." He felt she had the talent of a William Blake and he didn't want to disturb the flow and development of her intuitive vision with his academic ideas about "visual language" – his theory that all painting was constructed of collisions and transitions. Kris also painted with Liv in her part of the studio. Liv painted mostly landscapes using a dark, somber palette. Kristine used a brighter palette for her non-representational female figures. The two women challenged each other in their work.

Jan and Liv had recommended the Gnostic church Mass to Kristine. Like the Pagans of old, she had been deeply scarred by her Catholic upbringing–raised to cultivate self-loathing. Now she was trying to heal from having drunk at the fountain of guilt and shame. The Gnostic Mass had all the magic and mystery that she'd loved as a child, but it refrained from rebuke. One of the congregants at the Ecclesia Gnostica liked to call the Gnostic church "Catholic Lite."

# Sacrament of Confirmation

Near the end of September 1991, I sat in the rickety chairs of the Gnostic church after Mass, sipping cheap white wine with Liv Saether. We laughed about how she and I were the only mothers of young children in that weird congregation of heretical misfits.

Just then, Bishop Stephan came up, pulled a chair around from the row in front of us, and sat down. "Now about your confirmation," he said. I looked to Liv, then around behind me. "I'm talking to you." He fixed his dark penetrating stare on me.

"Did we talk about this?" I was bewildered, certain I hadn't discussed confirmation with him or anyone. After baptism, I felt I'd entered a long, narrow corridor and the only way out was forward, toward the next sacrament. I imagined I'd probably be confirmed in about a year.

"I think we should do it before Halloween, and I think we should do it privately," he said. I looked to Liv for some clarification. She just shrugged her shoulders as if to say, *I don't know, but I would defer to his wisdom.*

∞

These Gnostics celebrated Halloween with a fun and irreverent costume party. Pagans believed it a time of year when the veil thins between this world and the spirit world. From a Jungian perspective, the shadow is given an opportunity to come out and play. This congregation understood that interacting with the shadow could shed light on certain, otherwise hidden, states of mind. This was a time to openly allow opposites to mingle – to accept the unacceptable and recognize that what has been rejected is an aspect of the whole. Hieros Gamos – the alchemical sacred marriage of opposites, male and female – was given more sober consideration.

The party was always held on the Friday nearest October 31, Halloween night, in place of Stephan's regular lecture. Stephan would begin with a short talk about the deeper meaning of Halloween, and then set the tone for the daemons by exiting behind the satin curtains and turning off the lights. Spooky music would start crackling through the speakers, and shortly Count Dracula would emerge with plastic blood-dripping teeth wearing Stephan's great black wool cape lined with red silk. Dracula, whose Hungarian accent was close enough to Transylvanian, would emcee the riotous "talent" show. Jack-the-Bear personified a Southern Baptist fundamentalist TV minister; Serena – the rather large, middle-aged, pouty-lipped Czechoslovakian, vested in a nun's habit hinting sexy lingerie – promised that men's needs would be met by the sister of perpetual ecstasy; Judith would sing a show tune; and more. With potluck, spiked punch, and costumes that married religious themes with hellish ones, the party would go on into the night. It was a celebration that characterized the "outsider" nature of these Gnostics, able to find fascination and fun in the totality, the profound and the profane, two sides to one coin, a currency that has efficacy in reality.

∞

Bishop Stephan Hoeller was born in Budapest, Hungary, to Austro-Hungarian nobility on November 27, 1931, a Sagittarian. "I'm all fire and air," he'd say proudly. He bore the title of Baron, though he never used it. He grew up on a family estate in Hungary and was about thirteen when the Russians invaded Hungary, sacked his ancestral home, and killed his uncle and some servants, while he hid in the bushes. He left Hungary with his parents and spent some time at the Vatican studying to become a priest. In 1952 he immigrated to the United States and settled in Los Angeles, near Madam Blavatsky's Theosophical Society. Stephan was ordained to the priesthood of the American Catholic Church in 1958. When the first Gnostic texts began to emerge from translation, he left Catholicism for the study of Gnosticism. He was consecrated to the Gnostic episcopate by Bishop Richard, Duc de Palatine, on April 9, 1967.

∞

I'd seen many confirmations over the years, and they had all been done on Sunday morning during the regular Mass. I didn't understand why Stephan felt mine should be private and before Halloween. There was a sense of great import that he did not explain, which made me wonder if he felt I was in some kind of spiritual danger, particularly around All Hallows Eve. Was he concerned that the bad witch might crash the party and cast a spell on me? It was a mystery that the bishop seemed to have a handle on. I went along like a lamb under his care.

∞

On Thursday morning, October 10, 1991, I sit silently in the front row of the empty church listening to the tired recording of Gregorian Chants. Stephan and his two assisting priests, Jan Saether and John Goelz (Jack-the-Bear) are in the vestry changing from street clothes to vestments, preparing for my confirmation. David is there to support me, though he is losing interest in the Gnostic church.

There was a shift at this time in the tenor of the church. Carl Jung had embraced many of the philosophies of the Gnostics, and he conceptualized them as early depth psychologists. In the first part of the twentieth century, little documentation about the Gnostics existed. But after the find in 1945 of thirteen ancient Gnostic codices at Nag Hammadi in Egypt, more direct writings began to be translated. A new undercurrent was taking place in the church. When David and I began attending lectures and services, interpretations of the literature were largely psychological, in the Jungian vein. Now a mystical flavor had deepened the comprehension of Gnosis. I willingly submitted to this new rip current, moving inexorably out to the wide ocean of spirit, while David warily clung to the shore.

∞

A bell tinkles, and the three vested clergymen walk out to the front of the altar. Jan, gliding like a Viking ship, moves the portable kneeler to the center. The bishop speaks in a voice more intimate than the ritual voice he projects when the room is filled with people. *"Will the candidate for confirmation please step forward."* I stand and take two steps to the kneeler, not feeling anything particularly exceptional. I am beginning to engage in surrender to a higher consciousness, though there is still a hazy lens over my psyche. I am still not a full participant in my own life but rather moving forward in faith that there is a God who cares for me.

The bishop recites some prayers from the book that John Goelz holds up – the Liberal Catholic liturgy, from Madame Blavatsky's Theosophy, which Stephan adapted for the Gnostic Church. He lays his right hand upon my head and recites, *"Receive the holy ghost for the sweet savor of a godly life..."* He dips his thumb into a small brass thimble, which Jan holds for him. It contains a mixture of olive oil and balm that was blessed on Maundy Thursday, the Thursday before Easter Sunday. The bishop anoints me by rubbing the oil on my forehead in a little cross saying, *"I confirm thee with the chrism of salvation in the name of the Father and the Son and the Holy Spirit. Amen."* Confirmation is considered a baptism of fire because this chrism is combustible – it symbolizes the fire of the Holy Spirit.

∞

After the ceremony John Goelz emerges from the vestry in his street clothes. He reaches over to one of the vases of flowers on the altar and lifts a white rose from the bouquet. Lumbering over to me he hands me the rose, winks, and with an ironic smile says, "My condolences. Watch out for the thorns."

John Goelz, the senior priest, had been with the Gnostic Church the longest, I guessed about eight or ten years. Not over-weight but large and bearlike, he earned the moniker Jack-the-bear, no doubt due to his powerful yet gentle presence, feet sturdily planted on the ground. He had brown hair and a kind face with no outstanding features to peg him to a heritage. Not like Jan, who bore strong, unmingled Viking ancestry. I called him John mostly, but others preferred Jack, or the full and formal Jack-the-Bear. He had a murky past, ensnared by addiction and depression. I don't know how he'd discovered the Gnostic Church but it saved him. He had been able to lift himself up through study and the sacraments, myths, and rituals. He was well ensconced by the light of Gnosis; nevertheless the shady margins of life still fascinated him. He liked scary movies and even scarier Hollywood bars. He wasn't afraid of the more shadowy elements of the world, and his willingness to explore the full range of human experience gave him a rare wisdom and wry humor.

∞

We all go out for lunch to the local Armenian deli after my confirmation. The large, gray-haired Armenian proprietor always welcomes us heartily, calling Stephan "Da Boss." Stephan rarely speaks of religious or spiritual matters after a service. He prefers discussing the latest Stephen King novel or the virtues of Polish sausage. I feel a quiet joy participating with a group of people who can accept the painful dichotomous absurdity of life in this world. *Yes*, there is heartbreak so deep, loss so lonely, horrors uncountable. And *yes* we can still enjoy an ethnic meal, and laugh out loud, and mean it.

∞

The confirmation did indeed do for me what it was meant to do: *"strengthen the receiver in her determination to persist toward spiritual freedom."* The ceremony lasted only about fifteen minutes, and Stephan never did reveal why he wanted to perform the ritual privately – whether I was somehow privileged or in some kind of spiritual danger.

I felt protected by Stephan's spiritual muscle. I had an image of him standing, arms stretched out to his sides, holding open with all his might a spring trap door for whomever was able to get through to the other side – to liberation. From the book of Sophia:

"For he who shall give life to a single soul and liberate it, besides the Light that is in his own soul, he shall receive other glory in return for the soul he has liberated."

I imagined Stephan receiving glory for the souls he liberated through his staunch adherence to this ritual form.

∞

When I was nineteen years old, I had this vision: I see myself at age eighty-five, an old woman nearing death. I look back on my life, and my whole being sinks into despairing shame. I see that I'd been given this life to do something, but I had not recognized it and I squandered the opportunity, spending a whole life on superficial and irrelevant concerns. All is laid waste. Meaning melts into disgrace at my indolence and reckless wastefulness.

∞

At the time of this vision, I did not remember wanting to live like Jesus Christ. But this nineteen-year-old vision was a spiritual check-in with my greater self. It caused me to vow with every cell in my being to be true to the purpose of my life. I had no tangible understanding of what that might be, but I knew for certain that I had to be open to it from moment to moment, so that when all the moments were added up I would not end up inside that cautionary vision.

∞

The word *Gnosis* is Greek and signifies direct insight fueled not by facts and rationalism but by a cosmos of resonance that shows itself to be real, much the way a full moon on a cloudless night shows itself without doubt. The Gnostic mythos holds that the world as we know it is an error, ruled by the Demiurge, a false god, with his ministers, the Archons. It is with great effort that we navigate through these Archonic snares to the true, all-loving, caring God. I instinctively differentiated the myth from the meaning of the word.

Gnostic thought had gone underground for centuries because of persecution. Having become occult, it mingled with other occult studies and practices such as astrology and tarot. When Stephan formed his church, he included various esoteric elements. As more and more actual Gnostic scriptures came available, translated from the Nag Hammadi Library, Stephan aligned more stringently with those. There were many Gnostic scriptures I simply did not resonate with. I did not believe a false god created the world, though witnessing the rulers of this world in the twenty-first century, I could certainly comprehend how that myth came to be – born under the Roman Empire. But the Hermetic texts and the Alchemical sensibility that had filtered their way into Bishop Stephan Hoeller's Gnostic lexicon drew me magnetically toward them.

As a child, I had been guided to live my life illuminated by The Man of Light. The Gnostic liturgy called this "the Christ within."

I had been delivered to Stephan's Ecclesia Gnostica by the Christ within, who counseled: *this will do for now; follow this process, it will hone you; this man, the bishop, can guide you.*

Even in Hollywood in the late twentieth century, deep wisdom is never less, and the radiant cosmos dispels the Gnostic flaws.

∞

At this time I had a strong dream: I am walking down a forest pathway with overhanging trees and foliage. I come to a clearing where a large pond is fed by a waterfall that cascades down from a huge rock at the back of the pool. Kristine is there, waist high in the water. Jack-the-Bear is also in the water. There are others, but I can't identify them. Kristine shines with radiant happiness. She stretches out her arms welcoming me, her face a beam of sunshine. "Baby. You've come."

∞

Kristine organized a collective show of women's art at Bruchion, Jan and Liv's art school, in November, after my confirmation. She named the show *Giving Thanks* in honor of Thanksgiving. She invited me to show some of my work, and I entered the large mythic chalices I'd been making. They were shaped so that when placed side by side the space between appears to be the profiles of two faces. I didn't know any of the other women and discovered much later I was the only woman who was not a member of Kristine's We-Moon group. Unbeknown to me, my presence in the show had caused a stir: "Who is this woman Hannah?" was the snippy refrain from the other women. Kristine's response was "She's my best friend." We had only really just begun to get to know each other. Kristine lives in dimensions that don't always adhere to common understanding such as time.

It is the evening of the opening, and the crowd is clearing. I am following Kristine upstairs to the living quarters where Jan now resides alone since Liv moved out with the breakup of their marriage. There is a small kitchen, a bathroom, and three rooms of varying size that change purpose as the need arises: sometimes office space, sometimes bedroom, sometimes both. The residence is always a meeting place for students, friends, and children. Kris turns around on the step above me and, giggling with childlike delight, says, "I'm so excited. Now that you are 'Hannah' we can finally be friends." Her Pagan visionary insight shows her that the fog is lifting from my psyche. The spell is being broken. My confirmation has given me the strength to take possession of my true name. A personal sovereignty sprouts within me and shapes a vessel for our friendship to flourish.

# Chinese Bead Alchemy

One Sunday, Stephan is out of town and Jan Saether is celebrating the Mass. I am sitting in the front row wearing one of the Laise Adzer ensembles that David bought for me. A bulky necklace of various ethnic beads – black, red, and gold, including some made of metal – hangs round my neck. Returning to my seat after receiving communion, I detect the strong scent of metal. I lift the necklace to my nose, thinking the smell is coming from the beads, but it is not. I glance around but see nothing that can explain the scent. Suddenly I am aware of that distinctive inexplicable numinous quality – that knowing that comes from another dimension concurrent with what we call "reality." I know the scent of metal is a kind of "reference" to alchemy – the philosophy of turning base metal into gold, symbolizing the process of raising one's spirit to its highest nature.

My senses are becoming channels of transcendent symbols. The Gnostic Mass often engenders magical occurrences. This alchemical "reference" seems to have something to do with Jan.

# I Dream of a Great Stag

I am lying on my back. Perhaps I am on a bed of clover or a patch of dense moss by a trickling river. Or maybe I am in my bed, the down comforter draping onto the floor. A great stag is over me, on top of me, making love to me. I don't feel his weight pressing upon my body. There is no gamy scent. His hooves do not bruise me. He makes no panting sounds as his love penetrates me. I feel no hormonal surge or lustful consummation.

This dream marked a time, as a stag marks his territory, of wonderful magic in my life, when symbols came alive, playing out their meanings, whether in my sleep or while awake. Ethel was becoming Hannah. The person I had attempted to be was beginning gradually to become the person I truly am, closer to the Man of Light. I learned that the stag symbolizes regeneration, guidance, independence, and psychic power. It is also traditionally a symbol of the Christ.

∞

King and I sit on the deck at the back of our house in the valley shortly after the stag dream. The evening is balmy and King casually strums his guitar, picking out notes to harmonize with a plane that flies overhead. David comes out carrying a tea tray with cups clinking just as I'm telling King about the strange dream. "I'm going to have to keep her away from the zoo," David quips as he pours the aromatic Earl Grey into three mugs.

King, still strumming casually on his guitar, seamlessly slides into playing the Simon and Garfunkel tune, "something tells me it's all happening at the zoo."

∞

King and I had found each other in the rock 'n' roll scene in 1970. He was a guitar player who could play slide guitar right into your heart and loins. The first time I saw him play, my best friend Sandee and I had been given free tickets to his Shrine Auditorium performance. I thought he looked like a rosy angel up on stage, his long black hair loose from its ponytail was a halo, backlit by red stage lights. He was tall and moved his narrow hips seductively, and his angelic smile shot a Cupidian arrow into my heart. But that was my Hollywood youth when "first-thought" was usually not "best" thought. Shortly after we met, we saw each other at a party in Laurel Canyon. We had both wandered away from the raucous crowd to seek refuge in a small wood-paneled loft with lace curtains. We sat talking about music we liked and people we knew in common. We felt a strange familiarity with each other. There was a pause in our conversation, and we both gazed through the lace at the face of the full moon. Silence grew dense around us, and the music from downstairs became muffled. The air in the room felt thick and hushed. We sat there just looking at each other. "Do you feel that?" King finally said.

"Yes," I said. "What is it?"

"I don't know."

It was as if the room rapidly grew invisible cotton fibers that filled the air, momentarily pushing the mute button on everything outside of the space we shared.

And then it receded, and the sounds from downstairs reemerged from their underwater quality. We never could explain that strange occurrence. Our initial sexual attraction subsided and we remained great friends.

# Making Love on the Altar

Another magical symbolism dream came to me shortly after the Stag dream: It is nighttime and as dark as Hollywood gets at night, with its ambient light bouncing photons chaotically from the innumerable sources of streetlights, traffic lights, auto lights, neon lights. A priestly masculine figure – not of flesh, blood, bones, and attitude, but made of love – comes to me, not at the altar but on the altar. We come together, male and female, man and woman; the animals that we are and the spirits that we are merge. Every nuance of our act upon the altar is filled with spirit and magic – the *coniunctionis*: the spiritual wedding, the ceremonial magic of male and female complete as one.

The love I experienced in this dream imbued my daily life with spirit. My inner world began to expand toward a cosmic beauty, moved on by more nocturnal dreams and waking visions. The rooms I happened to be in or the people I happened to be with were pale forms of existence compared to the love that was burgeoning inside. The priestly figure from the dream began to merge with the flesh and blood human being Jan Saether, the artist and priest who had seen my beauty at my baptism.

# Art Calls Deeper

"To practice any art, no matter how well or badly,
is a way to make your soul grow."

KURT VONNEGUT

A group of eight congregants and clergy mingle on the sidewalk in front of church after Mass. I approach Jan and look into his penetrating and receptive eyes. "I'm thinking of taking a painting class with you." My voice is tentative. I'm intimidated by the secret feelings growing within me for him, and I'm nervous about plunging into painting.

His face is both stern and kind. "I'll be starting a beginner's class next month, on Tuesday evenings."

"I'm not sure why I want to take up painting. I'm really interested in sculpting. But I feel compelled." The scent of turpentine that infuses Jan's clothing emboldens my impulse toward canvas.

"You learn a lot from painting," he says.

The sun on my cheek doesn't calm the uneasiness I feel speaking with him. We hadn't really talked much in the past. I am a jumble of completely inexpressible emotions. My attraction to Jan, born from my dreams, is too unformed even to flirt with. But the dreams are propelling me toward him, like a planetary movement toward an unseen destiny. Underground elements are heating up within me, roiling like lava, embryonic in their movement toward an outlet. The resonance of my dreams and visions about him now erupts in my groin and belly, running interference on our conversation. "I don't know how to draw."

His speech is measured. "You don't need to know how to draw for this class. We start with how to lay out a palette, and then the first assignment is to do a Mandala – that is how you begin to learn about collisions and transitions." He clears his throat, a Nordic bass rumble. "If you are interested, a deposit would be appreciated as soon as possible." I sense his struggle to keep his art school afloat.

∞

The new semester of painting classes begins in the spring. I drive south on the 405 freeway from the valley, my insides fluttering like moths around a candle. By the time I park my valley housewife "station wagon" under the railroad bridge in the commercial area, my whole body is shaking. I feel the landscape of my existence lurching toward upheaval, like a nine-point earthquake. My soul rattles with excitation and beckons me on. Walking toward the front door of the school, I know I am walking toward my authentic destiny. There is a quote from Meister Eckhart painted on the entry wall. As I step through the glass door I catch some random words at a glance: *and perfect faith; receive God's body at the priest's hands.* I stop short and stare at the opposite wall. There is an image of a winged deity I have been researching because I had dreamed of this very image making love to me, as the great stag had done. This winged being is dancing over and crushing a dark figure beneath its feet – the immortal self, destroying the artificial delusional self. My sexuality is being drawn into an alchemical caldron, filled with spirit. I am being lifted up from the hormonal cacophony that had once crafted intimacy, toward the sacred wedding, the Hieros Gamos.

∞

Jan approaches from the back studio and looks at me with curiosity. We are the only ones in the high-ceilinged industrial room. "Is this not the beginning painting class?" I try to make my words carry a confidence that my gut betrays.

"Yes, but not for another hour," he says.

"Shall I come back in an hour?" *Oh God, yes, some relief from this surging and broiling in the core of my being.* But Jan halts my inclination to run away, like a giant magnet holding me in place.

"No," he says, "you can wait. I'll help you set up shortly."

He sets up a palette of foundational colors: English red, cerulean blue, Naples yellow, greens, white, in the shape of the Kabalistic Tree of Life. I watch him, trying to look calm, trying to be calm. My whole body is vibrating to a frequency I've never felt before. It is a mixture of sexual attraction with the true purpose and meaning of my life – my longing to *live close to Jesus Christ*. I don't for one nanosecond believe Jan *is* Jesus, but we are two who direct our lives in his name.

∞

Jan taught painting and drawing in the classical tradition. He had championed figurative art at the National Academy of Arts in Oslo when nonrepresentational art was the *art du jour* in the 1970s. He studied the old masters, particularly Rembrandt, and upheld their aesthetic, eventually developing his own theories about the visual language and how to teach it. He preferred traditional oil paint formulas and often mixed his own paints and medium; a purist, he also stretched his own canvases.

He named his art school Bruchion, after the famed library in Alexandria that had burned down more than two thousand years ago. Jan intended the school to be a transforming caldron for the creative spirit. It was a place of refuge, struggle, discovery, and transformation for painters, musicians, poets, Gnostics, and wisdom seekers.

With his architectural artistry, Jan had transformed an industrial space in West L.A. – two large garages connected by an open patio, with an upstairs apartment. He'd laid handmade ceramic tiles on a portion of the front studio floor and installed multipurpose shelving that could accommodate various activities. During class the shelves served as a platform for palettes and brushes; they could also display finished work and showcase various art exhibits. A fountain at the center of the unroofed patio, between the front and back studios, also displayed Jan's ceramic-tile artistry. Even though the apparatus that pumped water was broken, students would sit around the fountain with wine glasses on the ledge, legs resting on it, for casual talk and socializing.

In addition to painting and drawing classes, Bruchion hosted poetry readings, musical recitals, and lectures on Jungian thought and Gnostic mythology. There were bawdy festive gatherings and all-night discussions. There were love affairs and the dramas of love, men and women feasting on and fearing the nature of the other. Bruchion was a satellite venue of the Gnostic church for the more bohemian inclined. I felt a sense of liberation in this atmosphere, whereas attending David's professional social functions was stifling.

# CHAPTER 3

# Entering the Clergy

# Bruchion Mass

On Sunday nights, Jan converted the front studio at Bruchion into a sanctuary and said Mass alone to a congregation of two or three. I'd been one of those attendees for a month or two. My Sundays became devoted to Mass at church in the morning followed by lunch out with my Gnostic friends. I'd then migrate to Bruchion to paint or mend vestments, or just relax until the evening Mass.

My attraction to Jan had spiritual weight and depth. All my life, I'd believed in the kind of spiritual kinship I felt with him; I trusted it. Though I had no assurance that he felt the same way toward me, I was drawing closer to the unexplainable quality of love that I'd argued for with Sandee when we were teenagers. Jan was a man who heard the call to which the Gnostic Gospel of Truth refers and that I now experienced:

*Therefore he who is Gnostic is truly a being from above. When he is called he hears; he answers; he directs himself to Him who calls him and returns to Him; he apprehends how he is called. By possessing Gnosis, he carries out the will of Him who called him and seeks to do what pleases Him.*

# Not a Fashion Statement

I once watched a dog of mine give birth to six puppies. After the second pup was out of the womb and licked clean, it tried to crawl back into the opening. I felt sympathy for the little creature that wanted to go back to where it was safe, warm, and familiar. After confirmation, I felt I'd inched further along the long corridor that I'd entered at baptism: There was a doorway in the distance ahead, but the door behind me was closed, much like it had been for the pup.

About five months after my confirmation, I realized that the door ahead, the next sacrament, meant entering the clergy. This is the first of eight sacraments within the Gnostic Church hierarchy, which somewhat correspond to Catholic Holy Orders. I was surprised – *I don't even like the clothes.* But turning around and trying to reenter the closed door behind me was about as futile as the pup's attempts to squeeze back into its mother's womb. The final sacrament of these eight would be ordination to the priesthood, and I had absolutely no inclination or intention toward that achievement. I was simply following the voice of spirit I heard in my heart.

∞

On May 31, 1992, Ascension Day, six weeks after Easter, Sunday Mass begins as usual with five clergy members – the bishop, a deacon and subdeacon, and two clerics – positioned around the altar. I sit in a chair against the patched plaster wall of the sanctuary, holding a 50 percent beeswax candle and wearing a black cassock. The week before Stephan came with me to Cotters, the church-supply store, to buy my own vestments.

Vested in a white silk chasuble, the bishop reads the Collect: *"... the joy of thy sweet cry has made us remember ... We rejoice as we ascend unto thee."*

The bishop places his gold pointed miter on his head and is handed a brass crosier, the heavy staff that comes to a spiral at the top. He steps in front of the altar before the congregation of regular "outsider" attendees – the lanky man who lives in his car, as well as the sophisticated bejeweled white-haired Theosophist. A chair is placed before the bishop in the aisle. Formally, as he he's done many times before, he says, "Let she who is to be ordained to the office of cleric come forward." I rise from my chair. Jack-the-Bear, performing the role of deacon in a white silk dalmatic, steps to me and takes the candle gently from my hand. He lights it from the flame of one of the altar candles and hands it back to me. I stand and take three steps toward the bishop, measuring space between physical birth and spiritual delivery.

"*Beloved daughter,*" the bishop intones, and recites words about being properly purified to enter the holy and ageless mysteries. Am I properly purified? I trust that if Bishop Stephan Hoeller is inviting me into his clergy, my purity must be good enough. He continues, "*Since we are about to admit you in due and ancient form to the sanctuary of the mysteries of the Gnosis, it is just that we should assure ourselves that you seek to be thus admitted only in full knowledge of the nature of the course upon which you are about to enter.*"

Full knowledge?! If I had full knowledge wouldn't I be sitting on a cloud somewhere, sipping the nectar of the gods, and laughing my head off? I am simply and naïvely following a point of certainty so close in my chest that only I can see. It isn't full knowledge. It is pure intuition and internal guidance.

There follow some solemn questions from the bishop: "*Will you strive to be worthy?*" and "*Will you strive to increase the light?*"

"I will," I reply.

"*. . . You have been admitted into this sanctuary not as a mere cleric of the exoteric church, but rather as a member of the company of the elect, which is the mystic Ecclesia of the Gnosis of God.*

"*Hear and remember, therefore, the words of the ages, which must ever resound in the chambers of your soul: 'If I forget thee, O Jerusalem, let my right hand wither! Let my tongue cleave to the roof of my mouth . . .'*"

No, definitely not practical to go back to the closed door behind me and attempt to forget. I like my tongue as it is, and I am right-handed. I'm experiencing a mystical opening in the center of my being, which is calling me into it. There are those who might be able to dismiss a calling like this, and reduce it to nothing but a weird dream or anomaly, just heartburn, but I cannot disregard it. "Many are called, few are chosen."[1] I believe many are called and few choose to answer.

Jan and Jack, two seasoned ritualists, step soberly to me and place a surplice, the short white muumuu-type garment, over my head. Ceremonies are sober events, and Jack suspends his whimsical, sardonic humor during services. Jan also wears his stern Norwegian expression – a slight vertical crease between his pale brows – reserved for Mass and other Gnostic rituals. Calling down the mystical Christ to dwell in us is no flimsy undertaking, and Stephan upholds a rigorous standard of behavior around the altar.

The bishop continues, *"I clothe thee with the vesture of holiness ... that this white vesture may one day change into the robe of glory."*

My dream of the eagle that had perched on the faucet in my bathroom jumps into memory. The robe of glory is the grand culmination of the ancient Gnostic text called the *Hymn of the Pearl*. It is an allegory of the being who has fallen asleep in the world and forgotten her soul's purpose:

---

Call to mind that thou art a son of kings!
See the slavery whom thou servest!
Remember the pearl,
for which thou was sent to Egypt!
Think of thy robe,
and remember thy splendid toga,
which thou shalt wear and (with which) thou shalt be adorned,
when thy name hath been read out in the list of the valiant.

HYMN OF THE PEARL

---

[1] Matthew 22:14

These ordinations serve to remind me of my soul's purpose in this life. I might have some design differences with this 50/50 cotton-poly surplice, but returning to my heavenly home, clothed in the mystical robe of glory, is resonant with the deeper meaning that has always been there, just beneath the membrane of my awareness — *to try to live as much like Jesus Christ as you can.*

The bishop's goatee-with-no-mustache slightly twitches now as he breathes onto my head and says, *"I breathe upon thee the spirit of the mysteries of the Gnosis, and I communicate to thee the secret of the most holy name."* He whispers some ancient vowels into my ear.

When the service ends, I follow the clergy members back through the white satin curtain to the cluttered room behind the altar. The dichotomy between the sanctity that we reach for in the Mass and the nature of our surroundings bolsters the Gnostic mythology that purports the world to be a faulty place. The plaster on the walls and ceiling are crumbling, and the old sink drips, tattooing black blotches where the enamel is being worn away. The small droning refrigerator has lost its freezer door, and a block of ice dominates the upper third of the interior.

The clergy stands silently, honoring the ritual that is just concluding. Jack-the-Bear leans toward me and whispers, his vestments swishing silk against silk: "Bow when you cross the altar and snuff the candles in reverse." I'm not sure what forward is, though I've seen these candles being lit and extinguished for over a decade. Some new balance now moves within me, displacing old fears and nervousness. I reemerge from behind the white silk curtains alone, stepping smoothly, assuredly, and snuff one candle after the other, as if I have done it for decades. I return to the back room, where the clergy now whispers and smiles. We line up, lowest in rank first (me) and stride out through the curtains to cross the altar and disappear into the vestry.

The vestry is a twelve-by-eight-foot structural addition flanking the sanctuary at the back corner of the storefront, made of two-by-fours and plywood. Boxes of candles made of 50 percent beeswax as is prescribed by tradition are stacked on shelves next to a box of cylindrical packets of dissolving wafers. A clothes rack holding vestments in various colors for different seasons takes up a large portion of the space. Gradually we return to secular consciousness from the "altered state" that the Mass engenders, as we change our attire from vestments to street clothes without bashfulness; we are elbows to ribs in the tiny quarters.

Stephan, grinning his little-teeth grin, places his hands on my shoulders and smiles affectionately, "you're a born ritualist." I was never much in favor of routine or tradition; however, more than rote actions, the Mass now serves to stabilize a quality of presence within me.

When we are all dressed in street clothes, munching on store-bought cake and sipping cheap white wine, Jan comes up to me and says, "Bring your vestments tonight. You can serve." I look up at him with surprise. "You're a cleric now," he says, with an azure twinkle. "I can use your help."

$$\infty$$

Shortly after the ceremony, I came to Stephan's one-bedroom apartment in the Hollywood foothills to meet with him. He greeted me at the door casually and when I entered, Bobbie called out hello from the back room but didn't show herself. We sipped Turkish coffee, set out on the garage-sale coffee table and sat across from each other surrounded by books on most of the walls. He casually suggested that John Goelz be "in charge" of me – be my guide through the ropes. I could tell that Stephan intuited something might arise between Jan and I, and I think he wanted to avoid it. He knew Jan had a hankering for the ladies and, well, I was a lady. But spirit has its own intentions and though John and I became good friends there was no amount of protocol that could have prevented what was to come.

∞

David became very resistant to my activities with the church and with Jan at Bruchion. Like a male animal, he bristled at another male in my field. I was by then a card carrying Valley Housewife with two children and a station wagon. Sophia was twelve, and our second child, Dickon, was three. Both children aligned with David emotionally, and the fibers of our family were beginning to tear apart. They didn't comprehend the spiritual hurricane that was ripping me apart, and I was blamed and shamed.

One afternoon before I became involved with the Gnostic church, I was out doing housewife errands and pulled into the parking lot of a home-improvement store. I parked my car on the burning, midsummer tarmac, and as I walked toward the electric doors to the air-conditioned vastness of nuts, bolts, and lawn chairs, I passed a store employee. He was setting up some potted plants under a mister at the front of the store and boldly singing out a familiar song, paying no attention to me passing by, "And here's to you Mrs. Robinson, Jesus loves you more than you will know."[2]

When I married David, I took his last name, Robinson. I was then Mrs. Robinson. Spirit often speaks to me through seemingly random incidents like this, which reveals an open portal to "presence" eternal. Occurrences like this are always guidance for something I'm puzzling through, or just a message from spirit to remind me of who I am and where I belong. Carl Jung called this synchronicity. I've recalled this experience over the years, and each time it is a real and comforting reminder of my purpose in this life.

[2] Lyric from album *Bookends* by Simon and Garfunkel

# Mantis

As I move through the corridor/birth canal generated by the sacraments at the Gnostic church, the discord in my home life heats up.

I am alone, sitting on the carpeted floor of my study in the guesthouse on our property, attempting to draw my left hand with my right, from the exercises in *Drawing on the Right Side of the Brain*.[3] I am daring to move deeper into that part of me that must create. David isn't home, and the kids are in the main house watching TV.

Nothing in the air changes to signal another dimension, but suddenly I hear a male voice speaking: *"Now is when you will know that you are a Gnostic."*

The voice is coming from outside of me only I'm not hearing it with my ears. It reminds me of the *Superman* movie when Marlon Brando speaks to his son from "somewhere else." I feel no fear but I don't want to just buckle in wonderment – *wow, a voice from "somewhere else."*

*"I need confirmation of this,"* I affirm silently, and my thought passes through the same atmosphere from which the speaker's voice comes. I am certain that a sound mind wouldn't trust any old voice coming from "somewhere else." Bishop Stephan Hoeller often advised, "If you encounter a ghost, ask its name." But this doesn't feel like a ghost: the air isn't chilled; my skin doesn't have gooseflesh; I feel no fear. Still, I want some kind of verification, another leg for balance – like the second strand of DNA that stabilizes the whole. I continue drawing. I am green to this type of occurrence, and yet something in me is totally confident that hearing a voice speaking to me from "somewhere else" is not an indication of insanity, but rather a signpost leading toward greater sanity. It feels as familiar as a neighbor walking in and saying, "Potluck next Saturday."

[3] Betty Edwards

The next day I almost forget about my demand for confirmation. Late in the day, I am in my study when Dickon, who has been playing with the dogs in the yard, calls to me at the back door.

"Mommy, come look at this."

I push through the screen door, and he is standing very still, pointing to his tiny tricycle that is lying on its side under an old bent peach tree near the fence. I look closer and see a large praying mantis. I become alert and reverent; I've never seen one in the valley. I've loved them, ever since reading Laurens van der Post's account of the Bushmen mythology.[4] In their mythos, Mantis is a kind of Christ-like god, who has two wives. One of his wives is a rock rabbit who scurries about gathering food and tending to the nest. The other wife is a speck of the rainbow, a dazzling consort. I relate to that myth and place myself as the speck of the rainbow, not the rock rabbit.

Now, in the presence of this praying mantis, I have a sense of awe. Dickon and I watch her for a moment; she is very still. I assume this is a female creature, because it is said that the females eat the males after mating. The dogs sense something interesting is happening, and as they approach I ask Dickon to take them into the house so they won't hurt it. When the commotion recedes, and I am sure Dickon will stay in the house with the dogs, a palpable silence surrounds the mantis and me, and I feel a communion with the creature. I am moved to receive something from her, and I put my hand slowly toward her. Suddenly she goes into motion, as if on a mission, and strides onto my hand. There is a quality of purpose to her motion that is "more than insect." She continues straight up my arm, onto my hair, and settles on my forehead. I resist the temptation to cringe, and as I relax I begin to hear her talking to me. There is a flow of words that I sense is important. With the mantis still on my forehead, I slowly move back into my study for paper and pen, to write down what she is saying. This is what I am able to transcribe:

[4] *The Heart of the Hunter*

Here I am a bug and you are a human. Elsewhere it is different. Long ago and far away, one sees the unknown. Let it be known through thyself and others who know the self as one on the journey through and to eternity. One welcomes tragedy forthcoming of oneness in those who do not know. In inhibition lies danger. I am thyself forthcoming. Only for those who know the self as one. The corridor of fear is not where you belong. Essential love forthcoming. Though we die, we live in eternity. All being of one kind – essential love. Sinister reason has no place here, all becoming brethren of the light one. Sinister reason consumes the fire. All becoming. Advance notice of preparation. Sinister reason invades. Be with the one at all times, forthcoming. Put not your trust in men and women; they carry falseness with truth.

A numinous poetic atmosphere is present. When she stops speaking, I put my hand to my forehead and she moves back onto my hand. I noticed earlier something like a piece of her flesh dangling from her hind leg. Now she begins to chew on that appendage as one might bite off a fingernail. My heart is excited: she is biting off this flange as a gift for me! Mantis is giving me a gift of herself, like the body of Christ.

The following day, my rational mind begins to doubt the veracity of the experience. I do not make the connection that this might be the confirmation I'd asked for about the voice that said, "Now is when you will know you are a Gnostic."

A book of Rumi translations by Coleman Barks sits on my coffee table. A Persian man in a Persian bookstore on Westwood Boulevard once told me that they use Rumi poetry for divination. He picked up a book and slid a very long thumbnail between the leaves of the closed book. He did this three times, and on the third time he opened the book where his thumbnail had randomly landed.

"Then you just read from those pages," he said. "You'll know which words are speaking to the question in your heart."

I pick up the book of Rumi poems from my table with my head doubting and my heart looking for confirmation. Am I just making all this up? I run my thumbnail down the leaves of the book as the Persian man had done and open to:

"No wine glasses here, but wine is handed around

No smoke, but burning

Listen to the unstruck sounds

And what sifts through that music"[5]

I comprehend this poem by means of paired "presence": the resonance between my experience and the "random" choice of poem. This is what "gnosis" means for me. It confirms my experience with the praying mantis to be "real" and encourages me to trust and keep faith. On the side of a little round wooden box with a Celtic design, I write the Rumi poem with permanent pen and place the piece of Mantis inside, to keep as a medicine woman keeps her medicine bundle.

Shortly after this, I wrote a letter to Sir Laurens van der Post. I'd read several of his books about his many adventures, and particularly loved his expedition into the Kalahari dessert to find the truly aboriginal Bushmen. He was a friend of Carl Jung and was one of the thinkers and authors many of the Gnostics admired. His book *The Heart of the Hunter*, about deciphering the mythology of the African Bushman, prompted me to write to him. I told him of my experience with Mantis. He was quite old by then, living in London after a life as a farmer, soldier, and explorer in South Africa. I mentioned to Stephan that I'd written the letter. He was skeptical that Sir Laurens would reply. "Bobbie wrote to him and she never received a response." To my surprise I did get a reply:

[5] Rumi: *The Big Red Book: The Great Masterpiece Celebrating Mystical Love and Friendship,* translated by Coleman Barks

27 August 1994

Dear Mrs. Robinson,

Thank you very much for the letter and its astounding contents. I'm so glad that they seem to have the meaning for you, which I feel intuitively, whoever created the pattern intended them to have.

I wish I could write to you at length about it, but I am too overwhelmed with my work, and I hope you will understand that I can do no more than say thank you, and tell you what a great deal the myth and the personal story you have told me meant to me.

Yours sincerely,
Laurens van der Post

# Michael Manifest

Holy Saturday is traditionally a day for performing baptisms, when fire and the baptismal font are blessed. There was a well-dressed, stylish gentleman present who had requested baptism. I wondered how he knew about this quirky little church. I watched him walk to the portable kneeler and slide to his knees onto the cushioned bar. (I performed little cloth-related offerings for the church when needed, and I'd recently reupholstered the kneeler cushion). He didn't flinch or fuss when the water was poured over his salon-cut dark-blond hair, though a small trickle ran down the back of his neck under the collar of his pressed white dress shirt. When he stood, his khaki slacks slid back into place betraying no wrinkles at the backs of the knees or creases at the tops of the thighs. His walk was measured as he returned to his chair with a lit candle. Gracefully he snuffed the flame, waiting for the smoke to clear and the wick to cool before gently placing it on the empty seat beside him. His hands rested in his lap, as a cat brings its tail to rest by its seated haunches.

When the service ended, while the clergy were still divesting in the vestry, I moved to the row in front of him and, twisting around, said, "So you've decided to jump into the river." I gave him a knowing wink and smiled.

He told me he was baptized as a child, "Catholic, you know." His voice was calm and confident with a slight lilt. "I felt the need to do it again, consciously. I am moving to France and wanted this before I go."

"My name is Hannah," I said, extending my hand to him.

"Michael Lafferty," he said, taking my hand. His fingers were long and straight, with an old-gold nugget of a ring on his right pinky. His eyes were large and blatantly blue, framed by eyebrows so even I wondered if he tweezed them. We spoke about Lawrence Durrell, author of *The Alexandria Quartet*. "His widow still lives in the province, not too far from where I'll be," he said. I felt at ease speaking with him, and there was something about him that was very similar to David: his Celtic complexion and fine features. I was a little sorry he'd be leaving so soon. He didn't feel like the kind of man that would provoke David's wrath or jealousy and yet I felt I could relate to him the way David and I used to relate, playfully, before everything got so bad in our marriage. I didn't associate his name with Stephan's many invocations of the Holy Archangel Michael, with his heavenly army, though I was yet to discover that this Michael was every bit a warrior. I learned very little of him other than that he wrote poetry. He didn't divulge that he was going to France to die.

# CHAPTER 4

# Doorkeeper

# Little Feat Muse

I am twenty-three years old, alone in the living room of my boyfriend Derek's house, in the Los Feliz hills. He's outside puttering in the garden. I put on an album by the band Little Feat and begin dancing by myself. Kicking off my shoes, I feel my own unselfconscious movements stirring up from my core. Lowell George sings melodiously: "Take my independence, with no apprehension, no tension. You're a walkin', talkin' paradise, sweet paradise." An eternal moment blossoms large and poignant, like when I'd asked myself at age seven, *how should I live this life?* Though I've been running a business with two partners, Oz Studios – a creative center for music, graphic design, and costume design – I don't feel a deep passion or commitment to it. *What do I actually want to "be" when I grow up?* At twenty-three, I'm not thinking about my soul's purpose but of more worldly considerations.

Veering from the prescribed channels by not going to college – no majors, no curriculum, no career counselors – I had to wing whatever progress I made in life. Yet I didn't know what I wanted to "be." I knew how to sew, and during the years after high school I actually attempted higher education at The Fashion Institute of Design in Los Angeles, but I dropped out before getting any official qualifications. Sewing was a skill I'd inherited from my grandparents; it was not my passion. I didn't feel gifted with any particular talent or ambition – not for drawing, not for music, certainly not for writing, due to dyslexia.

*I'm an artist without an art.*

Suddenly while dancing to Little Feat in Derek's living room, the answer comes – *I will find my artistic fulfillment by being the female inspiration for a male artist.* I don't yet know the word "muse."

About three months later, Derek invites Patti Mitzui, my Oz partner, and me to come up to his house for dinner. "I'm throwing some steaks on the barbecue," he says. "I've got some business people to entertain. You two are welcome to join." Derek is the American vice president of an English record company. He is hosting a dinner for their English attorney and his New York associate who are all in L.A. on business.

Patti and I are in the midst of working round the clock on costumes for the all-girl band Fanny. Their opening night at the Troubadour on Santa Monica Boulevard, to kick off their upcoming tour, is in three weeks, and we don't think that we'll have time to go to a dinner party. But by six in the evening, we decide to take a break. "We'll be better off having a real meal," Patti says, considering that we've been running on cocaine and Japanese fast food.

We charge into Derek's house without knocking. In my tight yellow velveteen pants, a small turquoise Procol Harum t-shirt, and Corky platform shoes, I am a long-legged woman on a mission – *whatever these people are doing here, I came for the food*. Little Feat is playing loudly on the stereo: "I have dined in palaces, drunk wine with kings and queens, but darlin', oh darling, you're the best thing I've ever seen." David, my future husband, is one of the people sitting on the sofa. As I swoosh into the house, he says to himself, *there's my woman*.

He'd had a precognition in London before he left for California that he was going to meet the woman of his dreams on his trip to L.A. Shortly before that trip he'd had an experience with a rather mystical man from the Micronesia Islands. They spent many hours together in penetrating conversations, and I learned from his account that this intense experience had engendered a transcendental state of mystical Oneness for David that lasted weeks, just before he came to L.A. Perhaps this experience influenced his responsiveness to me and allowed for "some immortal hand" to move his desire for change in his life toward my vision of being a muse. He had been feeling stifled by what he called "two thousands years of British Empire." He longed for a freer, lighter life.

Our relationship began amid magic, creativity, and controversy – he'd stolen the VP's girl. We were both moving toward what felt like our souls' purpose. But after ten years of marriage, we were living in suburbia; David was a lawyer, and I was a housewife. Our creative selves got short shrift.

# Ecstasy

MDMA was an empathogen drug that had been used by some therapists in the human-potential movement to heighten feelings of love and to help couples address marital problems. Outside therapy offices it was just known as ecstasy, the love drug. Six years before my baptism, before Dickon was born, in the summer of 1985, the DEA moved to outlaw the drug, and David and I thought it would be a hoot to take some while it was still legal – just for the sake of being upstanding citizens.

I wanted to blow out the cobwebs in the corners of our life together, to awaken us from the suburban sleep we'd slipped into. When we first returned to Los Angeles from England, at the beginning of our marriage, I supported us, working as a waitress in Beverly Hills, while David took writing courses to develop his craft in short stories and poetry. After our daughter was born, he returned to practicing law; we moved to the valley, where we became mired in traditional "father-provider" and "mother-nurturer" roles. I wanted to refresh and reignite the spiritual love that I believed gave birth to our relationship. I hoped we could reiterate our communion with each other and with the creative passion that had first inspired our union. Our sexual relationship had always been good, but I wanted the fire of spiritual love I still doggedly believed we shared, the kind of love I used to champion during my all-night romps on uppers with Sandee. Just before ecstasy was officially banned, we made a date for Sophia, then six years old, to spend the weekend with my parents in San Diego.

∞

It is midsummer in the mid-valley, with temperatures still lingering in the mid-nineties, even after the sun has passed the mid-day heat. A slight breeze tussles the purple flowers of the Solanum tree that David had planted near the patio. A green iridescent beetle motors against the large fig leaves at the side of our back garden. David and I are drinking tea and eating sandwiches at the patio table. "Let's take the ecstasy in about an hour, after we've digested," I suggest.

David has been reading Marcel Proust, and rather than respond to my comment, he chats about Proust's concepts of memory and guilt. "Memory is selective, which is very convenient; why bother remembering what you feel guilty about?" His face widens in his characteristic charming grin. I laugh at his joke, designed to amuse and divert attention from any personal association with the comment.

By the time I open the little plastic pillbox and place two tabs of ecstasy on the table, I notice David is a bit lackluster about taking it. He goes along with it, perhaps to please me, but I sense he is not wholeheartedly into the experience. We each take one pill with some cold tea and sit back to wait. There are a few early stars in the twilight sky, and the neighbor's dog rustles, collar clinking, on the other side of the fence. David is quiet. I breathe in the heavenly scent of night-blooming Jasmine, anticipating the channels of love that will open between us.

"Do you want to take in the tea tray while I water the roses," David says, more like a directive than a request.

I do take the tea tray into the kitchen and then put some music on the stereo. David had rigged up some outdoor speakers on the side porch where I work on the potter's wheel, as well as on the back patio, where we take most of our summer meals. I choose Sade, an album I've been listening to while making pottery. Her steamy sensuality heightens my love sense.

David returns to the patio table with a glass of water, and I sit across from him as Sade sings languid and lovingly, "Your love is king…" I begin to feel the effects of the ecstasy: a quality of Oneness with all things; the wonder of the natural world and myself in it. I gaze toward him over the glass of water and seek that golden strand of connection with him that the music and the ecstasy open in me.

"Can I have a sip?" I extend my right hand toward the glass his hand is wrapped around.

"It has some whiskey in it."

"Whiskey? That's going to put a damper on your trip."

"It's just a half shot in a lot of water. I just like the taste."

My heart expands. Love lubricates every cell of my body. I'm breaking through the everydayness of life, dissolving into divine, yes, ecstasy. "Are you feeling it?"

He takes a sip of his whiskey and water. "Yeah, I think I'm coming on."

I look up into the wavy sky and feel the rhythm of my heartbeat and the smile on my face. It echoes throughout my body – in my bones a smile, in my blood a smile, in my muscles, like jelly, a smile. David sits silently, and I let him be with himself. When Sade finishes, he goes inside to change the album. Now a choir of heavenly music pours through the speakers. His taste in music is much more sophisticated than mine – I choose pop music, he chooses orchestral. It is one of his many qualities that have always made me feel inferior to him.

He rejoins me as I glide in a densely gorgeous ocean of cosmic sound. The combination of the music and the drug take me to dimensions in my mind – familiar, safe, and rare. "What is this?" I ask.

"Fauré's *Requiem*," he says, tilting his head up sideways as I move closer to him. Standing behind him I place my hands on his shoulders, stroking them smooth. I lean down and kiss his neck, blending our cheeks, butterfly kissing his right temple with my eyelashes. Pulling my chair near his I sit down to be close and face him, touch him, commune with him. I look into his eyes, and look and look, for him. But the one I look for isn't there. In place of the man I hoped to find, a man who loves me openly, a man courageous enough to live by love, I see a man living a role – "husband" – whose eyes shift left then right.

"You looking for the mote in my eye?" he jokes, then shifts his eyes again.

I begin to reel. Where is my partner, friend, and lover? The one who vowed with me at our wedding to be true to himself, for only in being true to himself could he ever be true to me. Instead I find a man who is ashamed and hiding. I back away, then try again to find him, be found by him. But he continues to avert me with verbal quips and sideways glances. Why isn't he coming out to meet me, here where the roles of our dailiness are dissolved, where the portal to our soul connection is open, where we have the opportunity to be vulnerable with each other, as I believe we once were? Even though I ask myself these questions, intuitively I know the answer. It is as clear as a tall glass of water with only half a shot of whiskey. He's not living truthfully with me – there is some part of him that he dares not share with his "wife," some shameful secret that has defiled our trust. I can see this in his darting eyes and the embarrassed curl of his lips.

I'd had a recurring dream for several years from the time Sophia was born, and it is now reconfirmed. In one dream, the house was on fire and I was calling to David to help me put it out, but he was distracted and wouldn't bring the hose that was right at his feet. All the dreams were about me calling to him for help and him being either drunk, unavailable, or just plain refusing to help me. I'd spent years in therapy and dream analysis interpreting the David in those dreams as an aspect of myself, my animus – the masculine component of my psyche. Finally a new therapist helped me see that the David who was not fully available to me in my dreams might just be David, my husband. That interpretation was like a punch in my gut, but I'd held in those feelings of disappointment and never really processed them.

Now, even as I am uplifted by the ecstasy and the feelings of empathy, a sinking emptiness befalls me, more deeply than when I had accepted that the dream David in my recurring dream was indeed my husband. All is one and connected and love, yet I am alone without my man; David holds himself outside the oneness. I am like a playful child running hopefully toward an open field, only to discover that it is merely a wall painted to look like an open field. I cannot feel – not anger, not regret, not even disappointment. I finally realize that the great tree at the center of our garden – our marriage – has been rotting away from the inside, yet I have not wanted to admit it. I feel no urgency to trim it or climb into it, no need to pick its final fruits or chop it down. But my heart begins a slow contraction – not from wonder, not from ecstasy, not from love, but from David.

# Crystal Palace Dream

Spirit never stops telling the truth. Only after you are willing to hear it does it begin telling you further truths. On a trip to England with David, to visit his parents, a dream drove home the truth that David and I were made of different stuff.

I am in a crystalline cavern of prismatic translucence with vertical gashes of dazzling light and color. It reminds me of the scene in the movie *Superman,* when Marlon Brando sends his son, Superman, off to another planet to be saved. Then I see whence David springs – his ancestry. His heritage is salt of the earth, farming lineage, toiling over and tilling the soil.

The dream is showing me how different David and I are in our intrinsic soul structures. Who knows how many separate genera of human beings have populated this planet and intermingled?

---

Therefore, he who is Gnostic is truly a being from above.

GOSPEL OF TRUTH

---

# Below the Horizon

I continued living the housewife life for another six years. What else could I do? Get divorced because my husband wouldn't become vulnerable with me on an ecstasy trip? The architecture of our life together and our daughter's life was tightly established and fully functional: We had a decent home, my husband was a provider with a well-paying job, and our daughter was in private school. I did not feel provoked to change things beyond asserting the small independent comforts I claimed for myself – my pottery and Sunday Mass at the Gnostic Church.

Then, when Sophia was nearing her seventh birthday, I discovered I was pregnant. Sophia was excited to tell Grandma and Grandpa, who were in turn excited. But a part of my being felt trapped. In my soul I felt a large clanking key turning a big lock.

I first noticed a red bruise on my knee about three weeks after my pregnancy was confirmed. I didn't remember bumping myself, and the sensation when I pressed and massaged it was not bruiselike but felt like a crackling fire just beneath the skin. It didn't start to turn blue and then fade like a bruise; rather, day by day it grew bigger, darker red, and more defined. Then my knee began to ache. The physical pain, along with not comprehending the pain, plunged me into a deeper sense of not knowing. Where was the mother instinct I'd had when I found out I was pregnant with Sophia? Why was I so unhappy about having a baby? Why was I feeling so trapped? What other life could I be living if not this one?

The doctor gave my condition a Latin name, *erythema nodosum*, which roughly translates as "red spots." It took months to get a more accurate diagnosis: ulcerative colitis. At the time, it was believed that ulcerative colitis was psychosomatic and caused by stress. Mainstream thinking now calls it an autoimmune disease, while cutting-edge research attributes it to an infection of strange biological mutations. I wonder what its cause will be thought to be ten years from now.

The baby was growing, but I was wasting with constant diarrhea. If I hadn't been pregnant, the doctors would have wanted me to "try" steroids, but given my circumstance there was nothing they could do.

∞

*Day-O, day-ay-ay-ay-O, daylight come and me wan' go home.* I hear that tune playing over and over in my head and remember how my brother, Gideon, and I used to dance around the living room when we were little to Harry Belafonte's tropical voice coming out of the blue-box 78 record player. Now I lay on the waterbed in our darkened bedroom in the middle of the afternoon while Sophia is at school and David at work. My legs are as limp as unfurled ribbons, with feet splayed out. I barely make any impression in the mattress; the tiny mound of baby belly shallowly rises and falls with my breathing. A slide projector casts blue light onto my body from the dresser across the room. I've added this "light therapy" to the herbs, chiropractic care, massage, and acupuncture that I am using to address my disability, hoping for some kind of relief. In spite of my sister, Sharon, nagging me three times a week – "Have you eaten, are you eating, you should eat" – I have no appetite for food and am unable to draw any nutrition from what I do eat. Food has a transit time of about ten minutes. At three months pregnant, I weigh ten pounds less than I did three months earlier. I am seized from my hips to the bottoms of my feet by a gripping pain. I am losing freedom of mobility and feel helpless, grasping at alternative healthcare straws.

I want more air, more mobility, more freedom, but I'm unable to claim it. Tears stream down my temples, puddling in the crevices of my ears. I sob and writhe, turning my head so that the puddles pour from my ears, creating two wet circles on the pillow. The water mattress sloshes to my moaning. The pain is unbearable – or is it?

Suddenly, lying under the blue light, I have a moment of clarity – *daylight come and me wan' go home.* The physical pain is transmuting. Yes, my hips are stiff and my walk stilted. But this isn't the kind of relentless nerve pain that is only relieved by narcotics. I discover that, by just lying still on my back – like a yogi – the pain vanishes.

So what is the source of this torment? Why can I not stop crying? Where is my happiness about this new baby growing inside me? The image of a tiger, pacing in a cage at the zoo with frantic, wild yellow eyes, comes to mind. Am I really that desperate?

My mind has been able to suppress the truth, but my body does not lie. It has given me a distress signal, S-O-S. I have acquiesced to this life, like a computer reverts to default coding when not given clear reprogramming code, but my soul has never stopped longing for something more.

The day of our wedding – May 1, 1976 – David wrote me a poem with a little doodle drawing on a piece of cardboard. The last line of the poem was "May Day, May Day, my arm around my bride." It was only years later that I recognized the double entendre in his doubling of the words "May Day," the universal distress call. Reading that poem on the day of our wedding and subsequent times I'd find it in my desk drawer, I'd only thought of the Pagan celebration on the first day of May. I had believed we were setting sail as life partners on a journey of deepening love; David must have felt he was becoming trapped, as I felt now.

# Mind-Body Connection

David was distraught about my illness. He consulted with our family doctor, who was a chiropractor and acupuncturist and had over the years become a family friend. He had told us about a unique hypnotherapist in San Diego County who was having success with a variety of health issues, both physical and psychological. David suggested I try going to him and I agreed.

Dr. Joseph Spear's office was not far from my parents' home. For several months, every week or so, I would drive down the 405 freeway, stay overnight with my parents, and receive two or three sessions in the course of two days.

Dr. Spear ushers me into a small room. I slip off my tan clogs and sit back into a black leather recliner. He unfolds a small blanket from the arm of the chair and spreads it over me. He places headphones over my ears, works the lever at the side of the chair to recline the back and lift the leg rest, and leaves the room. I close my eyes and begin to take slow, steady, deep breaths. I become familiar with the procedure. Calming music is piped directly to the top center of my head through the earphones as I relax in the black leather recliner. Then the fatherly voice of Dr. Spear comes through the headset, "deeper, deeper … And now as the adult you are … Going deeper to age twelve … There is a path … Comes a door … You enter the door and you see … And now deeper … As the adult you are … Age five … What do you see?"

Answering him, my voice is piped through the microphone hanging unobtrusively above my head into the control room where Dr. Spear sits. "I'm sitting in the back seat of our old dark-blue Mercury. My father is in the driver's seat and I am behind him. My mother is in the front passenger seat and my brother is next to me. It seems that we aren't actually driving yet but still parked at the curb by our house. My father tells a joke and we are all laughing. I want to compliment him for the joke, 'Oh Daddy, you are so…' Time stands still. I have a choice. I can choose the word *silly* or I can choose the word *funny*. To my child mind, both are equally complimentary. I choose silly – 'Oh Daddy, you're so silly.' In an instant my father has turned around in his seat and is slapping my face. I suck in all the air in the car; my brother can't breathe, my mother can't breathe. My sobs of disbelief are stuck in my throat. My father is silent. And then my voice breaks out and my tears are undammed, 'hic, hic, waaa.'"

'You can't call your father silly,' my father says.

'I didn't know, Daddy, I didn't know,' I cried."

Years later my father confessed how ashamed he had been of his reaction. He'd understood in that instant, without the benefit of psychotherapy, that he had simply done what his father had done to him the time he had called his own father silly and was slapped for being insolent and disrespectful. His shame, however, didn't protect me from the visceral education I received that it was dangerous to express myself by saying what I thought or felt, with possible inaccuracy.

Under hypnosis I also recalled a scene from my teen years when I'd spent summers at a Jewish summer camp in the San Bernardino Mountains. I'd worked my way up from camper to CIT (counselor in training), to arts-and-crafts specialist to assistant program director. One day, I was strolling around camp with Avi, the head program director. The pine scent was still strong in those days, before smog from industrial San Bernardino crept up the mountains and killed many of the trees. Avi and I talked casually and generally, looking out for stray campers, trash on the ground, and messy bunks. Avi was Israeli. He occupied the large family cabin with his wife and children. He was several years older than I and in a kind-uncle sort of way asked what I wanted to do with my life.

I answered, "I don't really know yet, but I do know that I *don't* want to be a housewife, married to a lawyer, living in the valley with three kids, a dog, and a station wagon. That is my idea of 'hell.'" He smiled knowingly and, with that Israeli acceptance that leans toward resignation, he said, "Ah that will change."

"No." I was adamant. "I'll *never* live that kind of 'plastic' life."

I found other memories and patterns of belief in Dr. Spear's chair. I saw Gideon as both my protector and my persecutor. Dr. Spear asked, "In what ways are your brother and your husband alike?"

"They are really not alike at all." I dismissed the question.

"But *if* they were alike, how *would* they be alike," he persisted. And then, under hypnosis, I proceeded to list eleven ways in which my brother and my husband were identical – within my deep structures of belief, though perhaps not to others.

After I'd been seeing Dr. Spear for several months I began to put on weight, and the angry red bruiselike spots started clearing up. I still had diarrhea, but it was not so disabling. By the time I was seven months pregnant the baby was growing well.

"What's it like?" Sandee asked, over the phone. Though Sandee and I didn't see much of each other anymore, we were still like family, and family shows up in times of crisis.

"It's kind of like he takes me by the hand and walks me through the garden, which is me, pointing out various features. It's like I'm looking at myself without judgment or fear."

"We were pretty worried about you for a while there. So, hey, whatever works," she said.

The hypnotherapy helped me come to a sort of truce with myself about the baby, and tentatively my mother instinct began to return. I still had pain in my leg joints and walked stiffly, but I was able to put aside my emotional torment.

Because my pregnancy had been so challenged, I wanted at least to give the baby a peaceful home birth. Ever since I'd visited Sandee in the hospital when her first child was born, I mistrusted hospitals for birth. It was about two years before I'd even thought about having a child. Sandee was a good storyteller, and she told the visitors standing around her hospital bed about how the attendants had been sitting in the hallway monitoring the machine version of her progress, while she endured the contractions on her own in her hospital bed. "It's coming," she'd shouted. The attendants sat studying the monitor and assured her, "the baby is not yet coming."

"I felt between my legs and could feel his head!" She laughed to us visitors.

"Get in here!" she'd shouted to the attendants.

We were all laughing in the telling of the event when her husband came into the room wearing green scrubs that the hospital provided. With a big smile on his face he gave me a hug. "You want to see my son? Come on, I'll take you there." We walked down the hall, turned right, down another hall, turned left, and walked to the middle of that hall to a window. "There he is; the third one in the second row."

After I counted the little bassinets to the newborn who was theirs, I felt my knees buckle. My heart ached. I felt deep empathy with the vulnerable little being, made of sensation, who seemed so confused and disoriented by his strange new environment and by all he was feeling. I felt his plea, *where's my mommy? I'm scared. This doesn't feel right.* The doctors and nurses were confident he was healthy and whole. Of that they were assured because he was crying, kicking his legs, and red-faced.

Witnessing this shook me to the core, and tears came uncontrollably to my eyes. Instead of these new vulnerable little beings snuggled and comforted by their mothers, who they knew from the inside, I saw farmed piglets in each of the bassinets lined up for slaughter. I swore then that if I ever had a child, I would have it at home, surrounded by tender love and kindness, warmth and compassion.

I did give birth to Sophia at home, with the help of two experienced midwives, our family doctor, and a close friend to keep David on an even keel. Now pregnant with Dickon, I didn't want any further complications to befall the child whose vibrant feisty wiggling inside me was beginning to demand my love. I felt his aliveness, and despite my reservations about falling deeper into my personal "hell" – married to a lawyer, living in the valley, and now another child, I was beginning to really care. David was probably just relieved that we were back on track. I walked with a cane and did not have that "glow" that pregnant mothers have. My face still looked gaunt, but the baby was growing strong and had a lot of energy, kicking and elbowing his way around my womb. I continued to attend the Gnostic Mass on Sunday mornings on my own, and I believe the bishop probably included my name in the list of people who needed special prayers of help and healing.

I found a radical, bravura midwife who actually agreed to assist me at a home birth, despite the initial complications to my pregnancy, and our second home birth was as successful as Sophia's had been. My sister, Sharon, was there to help and she beamed, "You looked like a model demonstrating the perfect birth." We named Dickon after the beautiful nature boy in *The Secret Garden*.[6]

Two weeks after his birth, Dickon was nursing and I was recovering, but without the vitality I'd had after Sophia's birth. I was not bouncing back. Then when he was three weeks old I began to feel very feeble again. I took my temperature – 103 degrees. Within the course of three days, my hands and arms seized up, I lost my breast milk, and my legs broke out in painful red spots again. My mother came to care for the baby and me. Sharon spoke with La Leche League to seek help. She even nursed Dickon herself; her son was a year old and she still had milk in her breasts.

I was lost from myself and from the world. I had reclaimed a frail grip on my mother instinct; now it fell again, down into a rocky chasm where I slouched at the cliff's edge, so weary I could not comprehend how to retrieve it. On the other side of the abyss there was a vague impression of a life – my life. I felt helpless and alone and didn't know how to save myself. I had no physical or emotional energy – not even enough to muster desperation. Within the next three weeks I dropped to 98 pounds; the bones on my wrists

[6] By Frances Hodgson Burnett

and knees poked up from limp flesh, and my breasts were like empty sacks. My mother fed the baby goat's milk from a bottle. We'd tried baby formula but it made him sick. He was living up to his *Secret Garden* nature-boy name.

After a week with us, my mother needed to return home, and she took Dickon and me with her. Sophia stayed with David so she wouldn't miss school, and Susan, our excellent babysitter, helped out. I continued hypnotherapy with Dr. Spear, peeling the layers of my psyche like an onion, recognizing more and more how much I'd projected the unconscious pattern of my relationship with my brother onto my husband.

I've come to recognize that for me life itself is the most accurate teacher – "the Christ within." Experiences are the lessons, and for me they occur by patterns particular to my individual soul's needs. These experiences tend to repeat through different events and people until I awaken to the pattern, and by so doing am able to awaken to a higher consciousness. My recurring dream about David being unavailable, showed me one image and storyline after another, all with the same theme, patiently trying to get me to comprehend its message. I had unconsciously made my marriage into a facsimile of my relationship with my brother, who I'd experienced as both savior and persecutor.

Gideon, who was two years my elder, had always, even as children, felt very protective of me. Though we came from the same blood, I believe we came from different soul sources, and I frustrated him. He couldn't make sense of me, especially my independence and desire to get away from the fold. Growing up, he took out this frustration on me, twisting up the dishtowel when we were helping Mom with the dishes and whipping me, all with the pretense of playfulness; or he'd catch me in the hallway and ram his elbow into my back – again, as "play." I went along with it, screeching and laughing, and my mother, who would have stopped any overt meanness, believed we were just being rambunctious kids. This was a pattern that was formed when I was too young to know there was any other way of being, so for me it was the way boys and girls, men and women related to each other.

Similarly, David used to belittle me with what he would say is "just a joke." He'd make fun of my family, and if I used a Yiddish expression I'd learned from my mother he'd shout in a duplicitously "playful" tone: "No Jewishness." These are small examples. I have no wish to dredge up deeper ones.

My projection of brother onto husband was a phantom of my psyche; I didn't see my husband as who he really was but rather who I believed him to be. My soul's lesson was to uncover this illusion, as well as other patterns that prevented me from "seeing face to face"[7] – seeing things as they really are. No doubt David had projected his internal beliefs about women on to me also. Sadly we were not able to wake up from these unconscious patterns together. Had both of us been able to awaken together, the marriage might have been saved, but there had been too much wounding.

One night I had an eternal moment with myself looking into the mirror.

*I married my brother and I've seen that mirage for what it is. I can no longer thrive in this marriage. My soul must move on.*

# Art Saves Lives

The following May, two months after Dickon was born, I am home from my parents' house, still struggling to regain my life. I sit on the lounge chair that David bought, and warm my frail body in the sun. The jasmine is in bloom, and its scent permeates me like a faint remembrance of a heaven to come. I absentmindedly pick up a fist-sized piece of Sculpey from the redwood table at my side.

---

[7] "Now we look through a glass darkly but then face to face." Corinthians 13:12. Looking through the glass darkly is seeing the world through unconscious patterning. To see face to face is to see reality as it is.

The oil-based clay has pebbles pressed into it – a project Sophia has abandoned. I begin picking the pebbles out and dropping them by my chair to mingle with the gravel beneath. I press my thumb into the ball and, finding a pebble, wedge it out – again and again – while staring blankly, emotionless, at the dark green of the fig tree at the edge of the garden.

Eventually my fingers find no more pebbles in the wad of clay, and I begin to press it into a flat oval shape, onto the lid of a Tupperware container whose body is turned upside down in the sandbox. I hear the baby fussing in the distant regions of my mind, but his discomfort doesn't register as anything that concerns me. My empathy is as dried up and sagging as my breasts. Susan, our babysitter, goes to him. I absently pick up a Popsicle stick that has slightly adhered to the table by some sugary residue and begin to draw into the oval of the clay. I don't wish to draw anything in particular – I was never very good at drawing, which seemed so flat, so abstract. But the clay doesn't stay flat. I can raise it up and dig down into it; I can feel it, not just see it.

An image begins to emerge from my doodling, and I feel a twinge of delight. It is a relief of a woman falling backward off a cliff. But the woman doesn't drop down into a lonely abyss, getting dashed against the rocks; instead, there are clouds with large hands in them that catch and cradle her like a baby. I ask David to buy me some more Sculpey and I spend more time making pictures in it – pictures of my interior world, of hope and salvation.

# Everything Breaks

---

"There is a doorway out, but it is at the bottom."

JAN SAETHER

---

By August, I begin to have an appetite again. The temperatures are in the high nineties; I am warming up inside and able to respond to Dickon. And then one night, everything breaks. Laddie, our little border collie, whines at my bedside. I sleepily get my legs over the side of the waterbed frame and glance at the clock – 4 a.m. I head toward the back door to let him out, when Sophia screams out from her room next to ours. I divert my direction to go to her; in the dark it looks like she's turned around in her bed. I feel a cold chill run down my spine and turn on the light to see her in the throes of a grand-mal seizure. Panic runs through me – *something about her tongue.* My tongue goes thick as I scream, "David" and repeat "David!" I am having a hard time forming the word. I stick my hand in her mouth – yes I know now that's exactly what you are not supposed to do, but this is my daughter. I'm not letting her choke. I scream for David again and finally he blearily shows up at the doorway. "Get me a towel!" I shout. I feel her biting harder and harder on my hand and I can't get my hand out of the grip of her jaw. *Where the hell is the towel? The bathroom is only five steps from here.* Finally David appears, hands me a towel, and I am able to replace my hand with it in her mouth. Sophia is still shaking, but she is now over the crest of the seizure. I look behind me and see David in his bathrobe, leaning against the doorjamb, smoking his pipe – the casual stance of the sophisticated English gentleman.

Sophia returns to consciousness, the paramedics arrive, and we spend the rest of the night in the E.R. There could be dozens of explanations for that seizure, which only ever happened once in her life. Here's one: I was not willingly accepting the shape of my marriage and not courageous enough to close the door on it. This created a conflict in my soul, a tension that my body could not hold up under, and it rendered me unable to shield my poor little girl; she broke under the weight of it.

It took several years before I stopped waking up at 4 a.m. in a state of panic, losing my little girl, nightly, to some netherworld.

# Ordination to Doorkeeper

On November 29, 1992, the sacrament that moves me to the second initiatory step in the church hierarchy, Doorkeeper, is performed at the church on "the seedy side of Hollywood Boulevard" (as Stephan liked to boast). The bishop speaks with his customary noble Hungarian formality as he stands before the congregation with his gold-pointed miter upon his head. He holds his brass crosier with the hand that bears a huge amethyst ring. *"Let her who is to be ordained to the Office of Doorkeeper come forward."*

Jack-the-Bear passes me a candle from the shelf where the silver holy-water bowl with its aspergilla and other ritual implements of the Eucharist are kept. I step to the front of the crisp linen-covered altar, light the candle, and seat myself before the bishop who sits on his faldstool.

*"Beloved daughter, you who have been found worthy to advance at this time from the order of Cleric to that of Doorkeeper should be aware of the significance of the step you are about to take. The holy and ageless mysteries have always included an office of guard or sentinel...In the present form of the mysteries of the Gnosis the office of Doorkeeper is invested with a personal and symbolic significance."*

∞

David and I had begun seeing a marriage counselor. I tried to communicate what I already knew – that this marriage was over. But David refused to believe me. "We're here trying to fix this! We're going to keep it together," he insisted. I realized I would have to wait until he independently knew what I finally had accepted. I didn't have the strength to shut the door against the torrent of his will.

When we'd first met he'd taken me like a talisman into his possession, with the hope that I, a freewheeling California girl, would by osmosis free him from the destiny he feared: that of the London solicitor he had already become. He wanted change; he wanted to live the creative life that he had the talent for, and he saw me as the muse who could enable that talent.

But he was also doubtful and didn't have faith in either his own potential or in me.

"We each have to work out our own liberation."[8]

For me, David had been a messenger on my soul's journey. It was through him that some of my childhood patterns were exposed; and it was he who delivered me to the door of Gnosis. It was also he who gave me my children, as well as infinite other experiences, insights, and benefits over the years. He was a complex man in whom I witnessed much that is common to many men. Some relationships are only good for a limited duration. The kindest gentlest way when they come to an end is acceptance. That was a hard lesson for David to learn.

Eventually he moved into the guesthouse. I imagined maintaining life like that, where we were both present for the children yet had our separate lives. I'm sure it could be done, given the right respect and acceptance of one another. But we had not cultivated those elements between us, and the animosity continued.

I was closing the door on the past fifteen years, which had both sustained me and constrained me, because it had replicated

[8] Buddhist tenet

old patterns that no longer served me. As my brother had been my savior and persecutor, David had been my knight in shining armor, whose armor was never removed and always bruised me.

I could no longer do as generations of women had done before me – live an entire life of compromise. "The times they were a-changing," as Bob Dylan sang. I was being taken by a wave of history that was calling women to come to their power – to come out of their kitchens and domesticity to be fully human. A refrain repeated in my mind: *something has to be done*. Still, I did not feel my personal strength. I'd become like a fish suffocating on dry land, flipping and flailing for my true life. Was it history's wave or divine chance that the Gnostic wind came and blew me into the sea before my gills gave out? I would put my faith in the ocean of divinity; I would surrender to both its mercy and its severity. I would practice acceptance and learn the truth that spiritual awakening is a bloody birth.

∞

Stephan continues with the ordination to Doorkeeper. *"Will you strive to use your strength and will…?"*

"I will," I say.

*"Will you cultivate within your own nature such pure and calm emotions as are desirable and necessary for the performance of the holy mysteries?"*

Calm emotions. With tensions at home still very activated, despite David's move to the guesthouse, my emotions were like an active volcano. After a lifetime of repressing my emotions, now as they were erupting I was supposed to keep them calm?

"I will."

*"The Lord of Light keep thee in thy resolve, beloved Daughter, and strengthen thee in the Gnosis."*

Amen.

# CHAPTER 5

# Reader

# The Power of Listening

It is Sunday afternoon. Jan and I are talking in the back studio at Bruchion, sitting on the IKEA couch that smells of oil paint, before preparing for the evening Mass. I start to say something, but my words trail off in a wisp. He says, "Finish. What were you saying?" He waits and listens for me to complete my thought. Jan is not one who makes a display of chivalrous acts, like opening car doors for ladies, but just now he opens a deeper door for me, and walking through, I am in wonderland. This is the first time a strong, intelligent man actually wants to know what I think. Jan's capacity to listen enables me to speak. It allows my feelings the spaciousness to form thoughts; it makes room for my thoughts to develop into words, and it acknowledges my mind as worthy.

I have never commanded respect from the men in my life. Was it all down to my father's slap that shut me up? Was it my different "soul source" that prevented me from being recognized by my family? I never felt truly "heard" by anyone, so I never even bothered completing my thoughts. My brother and father thought of me as a silly girl with ridiculous ideas, not worth listening to in a serious way. My husband was so addicted to being right that I continuously had to agree with him in order to keep peace. My mother and my few women friends did not challenge me intellectually. My own ideas felt vague and insignificant to me when I compared myself to the formidable men I knew: Stephan, David, my father, who was a physicist. How could my thoughts gain any stature when there was no one to listen long enough for me to formulate them?

Now, as Jan listens, I express the idea that the Catholic Church's rejection of women and the belief that humans have a right and responsibility to preside over nature, are woven from the same yarn, based in fear of the unpredictable. And if the masculinized version of humanity were to sit in true observance and respect for both women and nature it would learn something deeper about itself and thereby become greater than the greatness it aspires to. Jan nodded, seemingly in agreement.

# Lay Lady Lay

I sat at my easel amid a row of students at Bruchion, wearing paint-stained jeans, a flannel shirt tied at the waist, and red-leather ankle boots. I was working on my second project: the Degas study of women ironing. The shelving that Jan had built served as a palette table for the removable easels. I felt a density in the silence, which was created by the students' concentration. Jan glided, surefooted, into the room. He was a deeply compassionate man, a priest, and also aloof – an artist/master. His passion was contained, not reckless.

Snap, click, he'd brought in a boom box so his students could listen to music while they worked. The otherworldly sounds of the Bulgarian Women's Choir soaked my soul and sucked me back in time to a month earlier, when I had listened to the same piece of music. I'd been sitting on the floor in my study, my long brown hair waving down over my doodles. I was filling in a Celtic line drawing with colored pencils, following the pattern up and back, up and back, traversing the province of chain-link design toward the center, where the divine Celtic anima and animus, a man and a woman, were intertwined in a heavenly embrace. The Women's Choir had made my heart beat to the resonance of Jan's essence, and I felt the two of us at the center of an organized pattern of life.

Now, painting at Bruchion, the choir brings me back to that moment. My soul softens now that Jan is near me in flesh and time. The music comes to an end, and he drifts in from the back studio and puts on another CD – Bob Dylan singing "Lay Lady Lay." I fantasize that he's giving me a secret message and then wonder if there is someone else toward whom he is directing his intentions. Simultaneous with my doubt about his feelings for me, another internal voice speaks – a feminine power with burgeoning confidence: *Oh yes, but not yet, not until we're each, both and together, certain that laying across your big brass bed will be an invitation for the Holy Spirit to enter and bless our union – when the chalice and the sword become one, and the alchemical wedding informs spirit and flesh that they are not separate but one divine emanation.*

# Ordination to Reader

"*Let her who is to be ordained to the office of reader come forward.*" The bishop stands before the congregation, brass crosier in hand, his gold miter upon his head. His High Church vestments, hand-me-downs from some Catholic auction or second-hand trader, are slightly threadbare.

I was getting the hang of the ceremonial ordinations. The word "ordination" comes from Latin meaning "to put in order." The process of these Gnostic sacraments is meant to help the novice put herself in order. My internal experience was far from orderly. Each time I approached a new reckoning – another sacramental movement forward – I felt pulled into a kind of psychic disorientation. Having settled into the rhythmic floating in a calm sea with the previous phase, a new and different current would roil me under. I'd become worried about my children and angry with David. Agitation reeled through my body. My homelife routines – making school lunches, driving the kids to and from school, putting dinner on the table, reading to Dickon before bed – gave me some degree of comportment. I read Gnostic texts in snippets and pieces. What was real?

I was guided by my faith, which had no footing in the material world. Was I becoming what David accused me of – a religious fanatic, a terrible mother? All I could do was surrender to the tumult and the tensions between my old life and a life that had yet to materialize. My passion for Jan *was* my original passion for wild love and freedom, and it swelled beyond even his ability to reciprocate.

I had two beacons of stability: the Gnostic Mass and the poetry of Rumi. The Mass was like a well-built ship, with the bishop as captain, navigator, and anchor. Stephan had been sailing these spiritual seas for most of his life, and he knew the coordinates. He knew where north was, what the various types of waves indicated about the weather, how far from land we actually were. Rumi was like a deep friend who, when confided in, gave the most profound insight. I used his poetry to divine the truth, as I had done with the mantis experience. Whenever I felt bewildered, I'd open a book of Rumi poems at random and always find some stabilizing wisdom.

∞

*"Beloved daughter ... the office of reader is designed to call attention to the training and purification of the mind ... Will you strive to train and purify your mind?*

*"I will."*

*Well, I'm in it now. I'm going to have to purify my mind. I'm going to have to "thrust away unworthy thoughts, impure, selfish, or base ideas, and most of all thoughts of uncharitable criticism directed against my brothers and sisters."*

My separation from David was proving to be a long and bitter ordeal, and I often had acrimonious and hostile feelings toward him. My once knight in shining armor had morphed into the ogre under the bridge.

A good part of the humor I'd adapted to with David included belittling people. My chameleon like nature had me colorize my humor to fit his, much of which was mean-spirited. He would say things like, "That bozo with the two fishes hanging around his neck? His Mercedes is probably leased." And we'd snicker together, knowing how superior we were. I was now learning to untangle myself from that which wasn't compassionate in me. Purifying my mind for this sacramental phase meant dissolving those traits I had adopted that were unsympathetic to the suffering of others, even when their suffering manifested as arrogance. Unworthy thoughts that I worked to rid myself of included self-denigration.

One of the duties of a reader was to read "The Lesson," a component of the Eucharist, to the congregation during Mass. I was able to read out loud fairly well, because though I was not good at oration when I was in school, I'd read to Sophia when she was little. Starting with very simple books, three big words to a page, I developed the ability to speak the written word. As Sophia grew, the words got smaller in size, bigger in meaning, with more to a page. By the time we were reading bedtime stories with chapters each night, like *The Secret Garden,* I had developed some skill. I wasn't great at dramatizing the voices, but I didn't have to do that with the reading of lessons for Mass.

Reading books in general was a bane for me. I understood I was dyslexic only when I became a mother of two children who were slow to start reading. While addressing their difficulties I learned about the spectrum of dyslexia and recognized my own childhood complications. When I was about ten years old, my family moved to a new neighborhood in West Los Angeles. My mother, who loved libraries, took us to the local library to get acquainted. Surrounded by books, my heart expanded. I felt a quiet joy, as if the books were emitting a peaceful sound like a trickling creek or well-toned wind chimes. There was bigness and potential; there was an abundance of stories and ideas. I didn't understand why my teachers had always said I had a problem reading. I thought the words Dick and Jane and Spot were perfectly clear. In junior high, my parents put me in a speed-reading school. Then my mother took me to the eye doctor, who gave me funny eye exercises to do. By high school,

I had given up on reading, because every time I picked up a book to read, my eyes would become heavy after one page, and sleep would overcome me.

As an "ordained reader," not just of the exoteric but also of the esoteric, I had to address the problematic relationship I'd had with reading from within my being. This was more than a technical glitch with my eyes or brain; this was a spiritual challenge. I would never become a scholar, but I did need to read some of the Gnostic material. I discovered that when the words resounded in my soul, they opened up for me, and I was able to see universes of meaning. As time went on, I was able to accept and even be grateful for my lack of scholarship, because nevertheless, I had direct connection with divinity. I've known many people who have the intellectual understanding, yet still lack the "gnosis."

∞

Jan hands me the book and I step in front of the altar to read the lesson. "The Lesson is taken from the Gospel According to Thomas."

*"If you know yourselves, then you will be known and you will know that you are the sons of the Living Father. But if you do not know yourselves, then you are in poverty and you are poverty."*

# Walking with Jan

Bruchion was in a commercial building surrounded by little shops and restaurants – Chinese, Hungarian – and a sandwich café owned by Balthazar, a large Argentinean man with a fatalistic demeanor, who loved to talk and claimed he knew a formula for winning the lottery. He won often, though no jackpots. There was a Gypsy dance studio across the street and a Pakistani-owned liquor store up the block. Jan was friendly with the locals, and interesting people seemed to gravitate to him.

I'd been painting with the other students all Saturday morning when Jan came in from the back studio and asked if anyone wanted to go to the Thai restaurant for lunch. Two older women students in the front studio had brought their lunch and planned to take their break by the defunct fountain on the patio between the front and back studios. Charles, Liv's current beau and an accomplished painter in his own right, didn't want to stop for lunch. So Jan and I went to lunch alone, together. Pushing open the etched-glass front door, past the Meister Eckhart quote painted on the wall, we also pushed open the teacher-student personae, which we maintained as an unspoken code of discretion. For now, whatever might be developing between Jan and me was not for common gossip.

"Do not cast pearls before swine."[9]

Stepping onto the street with Jan felt like stepping into a long forgotten yet immediately remembered flow. Though he was at least six inches taller than I, we kept pace with each other in a way I had never experienced walking with anyone else. It felt as if we were a four-legged animal, or perhaps a string quartet that had played music together since the beginning of time. I was in a state of attentive wonder, acutely aware of this energetic harmony in the simple act of walking, when I felt the back of his hand touch the

---

[9] Matthew 7:6

back of mine. I don't know why I resisted his touch, which held firm against the back of my hand, but I pressed back; love is also a test match. The intensity of pressure between our hands, back to back, grew until he broke through my resistance, wrapped his fleshy hand around mine, and we strolled like childhood friends into the Thai restaurant.

We sat facing each other at a Formica table in front of the picture window to the street; familiar faces passed by. A small, low altar, with tangerines, incense, and flowers decorated the corner of the room near our table.

We talked about the Gnostic myth, or rather he talked about the writings of Mani. Within the Gnostic mythos there are many forms. The early Catholic fathers used to say with disdain, "Those Gnostics make up a new gospel every day." (Didn't Jesus say, "Behold, I make all things new"?) The mythos holds a certain tenor about the world: that the world is in error, created by a demiurge, a half maker, not in the image of the true God. This is open for wide interpretation and mythologizing. Jan was drawn to the poetic writings of Mani, founder of Manichaeism – one of several branches of Gnosticism. I was drawn to the Alchemical and Hermetic wisdom. Neither of us really believed that the world itself is an error. These differentiations between the branches of Gnosis were a blur to me at the time.

The waitress brings two dishes of pad Thai and a Thai iced tea. As Jan shakes hot sauce generously over his dish, he looks up and says unceremoniously, "I can't really get involved." His eyes are an inviting blue sea. Even as he pushes me from him, he pulls me toward him, like two fish swimming in opposite directions. "I'm planning to move back to Norway. Starting a relationship now would undermine my intention." His words drift into the roiling waters of my heart and settle at the bottom of the sea like so much meaningless flotsam and jetsam. I am being burnt from a distant deep. I am the tiger out of the cage in raw hunt for the Sophia – Wisdom. This love that is growing in me has no designs on domestication, is beyond time and place. The condition of his possibly leaving at some undetermined future has no bearing. He is here now, and a longed for presence is igniting between us. Though Stephan had set me up to be mentored by John Goelz, Jan is the one chosen by some immortal hand to help guide me through the mystic corridor of Gnostic sacraments, like Ariadne's thread.

The next day while walking to the Thai restaurant with Kristine, both of us in paint clothes, she said, "Jan's been going back to Norway ever since I met him," as if it were just a pipe dream.

# Walking with Kristine

Kristine exuded a shimmery sexuality. It was always with her and at times it would balloon, unbidden, like a swell of colors flashing out in a dazzling display from a hidden source. She seemed totally ignorant of her effect on men, leaving them fallen in her wake as if hit by a felling angel. Walking with her sometimes made me feel like a Dodge Dart compared to her silvery Jaguar. Her appeal was innocent sexuality. It eventually caused a rift in her relationship with Liv, who believed that Kris manipulated men, particularly Jan, and also Charles, Liv's current boyfriend, who was also one of the Bruchion "Olympians." But Jan and Charles were like most men, bedazzled by Kristine's shimmer, helpless under her fairy-dust beauty, which promised eternal sexual fulfillment with every swivel of her hips. Other times when I was with Kristine, I'd feel her beauty reflected in me – two striking women in the prime of our creativity, independence, and sexuality – the decade of our forties. She would often take my hand when we'd walk together, like two little girl-friends. She was unwittingly teaching me how to be a girl. Girliness was foreign to me. I was more a lone wolf than an innocent child.

# Rodney King Sacrament

When you make the two one, and when you make the inner
as the outer and the outer as the inner and the above as the below,
and when you make the male and the female into a single one,
so that the male will not be male and the female not be female,
when you make eyes in the place of an eye, and a hand in the place
of a hand, and a foot in the place of a foot, and an image in the
place of an image then shall you enter the Kingdom.

THE GOSPEL ACCORDING TO ST. THOMAS

Kristine's home, part of her recent divorce settlement, was a large, open, modern house on a hilltop in Topanga Canyon, in the Santa Monica Mountains. It had no internal doors save for the one that was rarely closed on the main bathroom. Kristine was not shy about bodily functions – perhaps because of her Catholic upbringing. If God can see everything anyway, why bother closing doors? A vast redwood deck wrapped around two sides of the house, and the view swept down the mountains to Santa Monica and parts of West L.A. A large hammock hung from a eucalyptus tree near a wooden hot tub. The house was planted on bedrock – a fact she was grateful for when the January 1994 earthquake struck. Generous Kristine made her home a haven for freedom and discovery. She hosted African shamans, Native American wise women, and artists of all stripes. With her pricey-but-livable furniture, her home was a kind of salon of refuge above the smog and traffic of L.A.

"Mi casa es su casa," she'd say in her little girl voice. Her friends didn't need to be entertained. They'd simply find comfortable corners in the house or meditation spots on the hillside, where they could breathe away the stresses of the city below. Visitors would generally find Kristine painting in her studio on the top floor. Kris painted from an interior place. Her figures were not anatomically accurate in the way Jan painted, but she captured the mysteries of feelings and dreams. Her palette and her line expressed vulnerability and sensuality. She seemed to have an uncontaminated connection to the source of creation itself.

I arrived at Kristine's house midmorning on April 29, 1992, and found her painting in her studio. She was wearing her black "beautiful-woman" dress. I had the same dress in wine red, and we both liked the way they made us feel like beautiful women. Hers was now stained with dabs of paint and torn a bit at the side seam, which only enhanced her beauty and sexuality. I sank into the posh, worn armchair, redolent with the heady scent of turpentine. She lit a candle on a shelf arrayed with shells, feathers, stones and paint tubes – an altar to beauty. "We will have to talk about innocence," she said. "It is just one of those places that you can't manufacture, but that somehow frees you by being authentically in it, which is why it is enough."

I took a sip of tea and glanced at a large painting of a female figure with doves flying from her outstretched hands.

"If you are looking for it, it is not enough, but if it is what you truly are, it is … like suffering and how it opens the heart, or peace, and all of these authentic places are of consciousness and wholeness, oneness, when you actually are in that one seat."

Jan once said, "Kristine would talk and no one understood what she was saying." But I comprehended her, because I listened to her from my heart more than from my mind.

When we finished our tea, I went outside to the hammock to breathe in the eucalyptus shade of the warm spring day, and my thoughts drifted.

I feel a presence and open my eyes to the visage of a knight with the face of another age: bearded, virile, heroic and chaste – a man of worth, a man of sanctity, a knower, a seer. "Hello." Jan's maple voice pours warmly over my body.

"Your voice sounds so familiar," I say, shielding my eyes from the glare of the sun. He's standing tall, relaxed, in white cotton slacks and a white shirt with sleeves rolled up, a few paint stains decorating his attire. "All my clothes, even the good ones, end up with paint stains."

He chuckles and slips with confidence into the hammock next to me. "Well you've heard my voice before," he says seductively. I breathe in his musk and become aware of my beating heart.

"But this is different, like when we walk together." We rock gently from side to side watching the leaf shadows swaying over us. "Have you seen Kristine?"

"I came in through her studio. She's working on that turtle-dream painting."

We talk for a while, then he slips two pieces of blotter acid out of his shirt pocket. We each take one onto our tongues: *The Lord be with you, and with Thy spirit.*

We lie side by side in the hammock, silent, surrendering to the sacrament now taking us. Kristine puts on some music in the house that broadcasts through the outdoor speakers. The Agape Choir sings, "I will give you rest." I feel my spirit expand beyond the toxic discord I've been experiencing continuously at home. The boundaries between Jan and me begin to soften, and we share an undefended exchange of energy. I don't think I've ever felt this at ease lying next to a man.

The Agape Choir ends and now birdsong penetrates the thick silence, while flies hardly bother to buzz in the lazy, spring-warm day. The house is quiet, and we move inside onto Kristine's ornate brass bed. Lying side by side holding hands, we feel the effects of the LSD coming on stronger, like an orchestra tuning up for a magnificent concert. I move to sit up and Jan gently tugs my hand, *don't go*. I turn and smile, *just one minute*. I fumble with the bedroom stereo in a cabinet at the opposite side of the room to put on a cassette tape that I brought. We lay in stillness now, next to each other on our backs, holding hands, fully clothed, listening to the warm Southern drawl of Coleman Barks reciting his Rumi translations.

The effect of the psycho-sacrament deepens, and love becomes fluid between us. The boundaries that define him, and define me, soften, diffuse, then dissolve. We now merge inside the Sophianic poetic spirit, one male/female. There is no sexual consummation; there is no ego. There is only a submersion into another dimension, devoid of fear, that is only love.

---

"If anyone asks you how the perfect satisfaction of all our
sexual wanting will look, lift your face and say,
Like this."

RUMI

---

"You knew; you've done this; you knew this," Jan says much later, after the effects of the entheogen have worn off. We are sitting in the living room on the brown-silk down sofa. His face is a sun of joyfulness and wonder, "I don't know who I am anymore."

I smile. I don't know how I knew, but he is right, I did know that identities – who we think we are – are like prefabricated stick figures in a wild rushing of eternal cosmic color and transmuting forms. I did not "design" this dissolving experience with Jan, but this is the wild Sophianic *Love, the observance of deep feminine nature* I have always longed for.

∞

"The city is burning!" Kristine has a dramatic expression of concern as she comes in carrying a tray of tea. "It's all on the news. Those cops who beat up Rodney King were acquitted, and people are rioting in the streets." We all go out onto the deck and see buttons of flame dotting the distance down in the city. Jan's school and home, his children and Liv might be in danger – they are all on the West Side. He kisses me and hugs Kristine and leaves in a state of heightened alertness, worry returning to his consciousness. My children are in the valley with David. I am not worried that the riots will spread to the valley.

---

"Consciousness is bearing the tension of the opposites."

C.G. JUNG

---

# Dance Me to the End of Love

Jan, still wearing his paint-stained apron, emerges from the back studio at Bruchion with a boom box smeared with oily fingerprints. He sets it at the end of the long shelf and reaches down to plug it in. It is Sunday evening and we are transforming the front studio into a sanctuary for the private Mass we now perform together weekly. I take my small Swiss army knife out of my purse and begin cleaning out the various brass candlesticks, two of which are decorated with cobra hoods that snake down to form the base; several small cheap Indian ones; and three brass candelabras, each bent or wobbly. They've been strewn about the room or taken to the back studio during the week. I gather them now and arrange them with new candles on the shelving along both sides of the room.

Jan stops to study a canvas that is leaning against the wall on the upper shelf, emitting the fresh scent of turpentine. It's a self-portrait that his teenage daughter, Elisa, has just finished. The eyes are poetically large, the mouth enigmatic – a modern Mona Lisa. Her style is a cross between Jan's and Kristine's. She has the formal academic knowledge of paint she no doubt picked up by growing up in an art school; and she has a feminine heart connection to her images, as Kristine does.

"She will be the one remembered by history," Jan says of his daughter. "I will just be a footnote – her father." I look into his eyes – bushels of sorrow and acceptance – and lift my right hand to his cheek – *your life is not meaningless; nothing is ever wasted.* He playfully turns his head and catches my pinkie finger between the cushions of his lips.

I smile and turn toward the closet to bring out the linens. Jan reaches up to the horizontal dowel that hangs from the ceiling, and releases the tapestry backdrop that defines our sanctuary. Our minds are quiet, our movements economized. We do only what is needed to prepare for the Mass. Silently, moving in unison toward the wall, we each grasp a side of the heavy wooden altar and slide it to the center in front of the tapestry, checking to make sure it is aligned with the pattern of the Persian rug. I walk around to the closet to get the incense stand and hear the click of the boom box. A melancholy accordion begins to play. I spread the starched white linen across the altar, and the scent of incense from last week's Mass mixes with turpentine in the still air. Jan stands behind me coaxing me around to face him. As I turn he folds me into his teddy bear embrace and begins to sway to Leonard Cohen's sibylline cave of a voice:

> *Dance me through the panic till I'm gathered safely in*
> *Lift me like an olive branch and be my homeward dove*
> *Dance me to the end of love.*

# Transformation by Art

---

"The great uplifting of humanity beyond its self-destruction
is the redemptive mission of art."

ALEX GREY

---

The changing form of my life was like a wild Arabian horse
pulling forward while a Spanish bull pulled back. Between the taut-
ness, I painted – dark blues and greens with splashes of English red.
Tufts of paint rose up from the canvas, as the image of mystic rose
petals emerged. A burning chalice hovered in an upside-down sky
over a cerulean cove peopled by strange beings.

Jan was an alchemist with color; he was teaching me about
the moods and mutability of oil paint. He'd skillfully reach his Viking
arm to a portrait, place a dot of white to the corner of an eye, and the
face on the canvas would bear a whole new expression. My image
of a chalice with tongues of red and orange flame at the rim, which
dominated my canvas, ignited when he came up behind me, cleared
his throat with a low rumble, and caringly took my brush to place
a thin line of turquoise, like a halo, around the chalice. Suddenly
my painting had more visual depth, and it erupted with what I was
feeling inside and wanting to express – a scorching feminine-sexual
spirituality that was making a train wreck of my old life.

∞

Jack-the-Bear sometimes took classes with Jan and Liv.
He depicted feminine images in his paintings – the Holy Sophia –
and was a good painter. He sometimes gave lectures at Bruchion
on Tarot or white magic, and occasionally did his performance art

piece impersonating a Southern TV evangelist – a more fleshed out portrayal of his Halloween sketch. With his baritone singing voice and his great ability to mimic the essence of those fundamentalist characteristics, his performances were always a hit with the Gnostic Society and Bruchion's anti-dogmatic crowd.

Once, when I was working on my burning chalice, Jack ambled into Bruchion and stood at my side. He looked at my canvas with dark, penetrating seeing for a moment, then turned to look into my eyes. Smiling a sardonic smile, his eyes widened. "Scary." He knew how coming closer to the spiritual fire wreaks havoc with normal lives.

# CHAPTER 6

# Exorcist

# Initiation

"The search for reality is the most dangerous of all undertakings,
for it destroys the world in which you live."

NISARGADATTA MAHARAJ

Initiate, initial, initiation – begin, to begin. What is initiation? *A shepherding process created by persons of greater experience to draw less experienced persons toward greater knowledge. Initiation causes a fundamental process of change to begin within the person being initiated. It means "entrance" or "beginning" – literally "a going in."*[10]

I did not know I was being initiated in an ancient Hermetic Way. I was simply following a single point of light in my mind through a world of shadows and crude patterns. I never consciously sought out the initiatory process; it came to me. I hardly even knew something that authoritative existed in our time; still there was a knowing within me that belonged to something greater than the lifestyle I had poured myself into. I had been imitating the world around me, a world that can be seen, when observed with the historical mind, to be increasingly coming apart at the seams.

I had never felt bound up by Judaism. When I told my family I was planning to marry an Englishman, my brother said, "I don't see what the big deal is. You never dated Jewish guys." I had never studied Judaism, as I had not studied anything with a passion or focus. I was that innocence that Kristine spoke of, taken up by some-

[10] https://en.wikipedia.org/wiki/Initiation

thing I trusted above all else. I didn't denounce my tribal bloodline; this kind of initiation, simply known as "The Way," crosses blood ties. Still a part of me questioned: *What's a nice Jewish girl doing in a place like this?*

Could I have made it back to the shore from this spiritual ocean whose currents were sweeping me out to a different life? I suppose I could have paddled and flailed and set up alarms. I see people running from their spirit selves all the time. But I sensed "essential love forthcoming," as confirmed by the mantis's message. My spirit was speaking to me, guiding me from inside. What would have become of my life if I'd ignored or pretended that I didn't belong to my spirit?

Beating a steady rhythm, like unseen drumming deep in the jungle of my existence, was the refrain *something has to be done.* Paul Simon's song *Further to Fly* became an anthem in my uncertainty. "There may come a time when I will lose you." *The initiation process is often likened to a simultaneous death and rebirth, because as well as being a beginning it also implies an ending, as existence on one level drops away in an ascension to the next.*[11]

In the Nag Hammadi Library, there is a mystical text called the Trimorphic Protennoia. In translation it begins, "I am Protennoia, the Thought that dwells in the Light." I was beginning to comprehend the mystical *knowing* that asked my childhood question *how should I live this life?* and the knowing that answered it, *try to live as much like Jesus Christ as you can,* was this Protennoia. This initiation was drawing me through what the mystery calls a metanoia – an about-face from the delusional world toward Truth.

This wisdom tradition now reverberated in my dreams and internal awareness. The Christian symbols that in our time have become washed out and Hallmark-carded, were growing new shoots and coming alive in me – symbols like the Divine Shepherd

[11] ibid

and being born again. In *The Gospel of Thomas*, Jesus says, "Put a hand in the place of a hand and a foot in the place of a foot." The juice of those ancient symbols were now replacing the shopping-mauled symbols, and were growing in depth and breadth and meaning within me. I was learning that there is a false demarcation between Judaism and Christianity. They are both of the Abrahamic lineage.

# Exorcising Fear

When I was five or six years old, I pocketed the quarter I'd been given as Chanukah "gelt" and ventured from our tract-housing enclave out to the main road, White Oak Avenue. I waited at the wide intersection, and when the light turned green for me, and the cars stopped at their red light, I crossed over to the liquor store. Looking over the candy counter, I selected my treats, paid for my purchase and made my way back home. I had no fear of the world, no thought about abductors, no concern for drunk drivers. I trusted the traffic lights to provide safe passage, but mostly I had faith in the preservation of my life. There was a light of protection around me. I had no need to fear.

I never got in trouble for my foray out to the wider world. I don't think I even mentioned it to my mother. It was just my world, and I sensed my world was much larger than the world in which my parents kept me, protected and safe. Of course I needed their physical protection, but I didn't need their worry and fear of what bad things might happen, because I already felt protected and safe by the light I knew within me. Still, their worry and fear seeped into my child-theta-unconscious mind and caused a contraction in my spirit. It is these subtle unconscious invaders that Gnostic Exorcism addresses. I needed to exorcise fear – which is also anger and bitterness, sadness and disappointment – so that my original Faith could reemerge and thrive.

# Ordination to Exorcist

Stephan is moving me up the initiatory rungs.

*"Beloved daughter," the bishop says, "... The order of exorcist asks you to strive to obtain a state of balance and peace within your nature ..."*

The Gnostic understanding of exorcism at this level is psychologically based. As I was not raised Catholic, my only reference to exorcism was the movie *The Exorcist*.

"I will." I am actually beginning to feel more balanced in my own nature.

*"Will you strive to ever remember that the exorcist as an ordained healer must embody the qualities of benevolence and wholeness and show them forth to the community?"*

"I will."

Showing forth benevolence to the community was easy, because the community reflected it back to me; there was always a quality of brotherly love amid the Gnostic milieu. Benevolence, however, was not the whole of me. I still harbored tremendous bitterness in my heart toward David, and the toxicity between us could make my benevolence with others feel false. He was living in the guesthouse and I in the main house. He was immodest in his activities with women, and it would get my ire up, because I felt he was using these women to deliberately spite me at the expense of our children, exposing them to his indiscretions while at the same time poisoning them against me.

I discovered that kindness begets kindness and sets a new patterning into motion – and faking it until you make it turns out to really work. I deliberately practiced goodwill, and my capacity for goodwill began to strengthen as my anger subsided. I worked to direct kindness to everyone I encountered, even if they didn't reflect it back. I've discovered that quite often people will eventually smile and soften when treated with kindness.

In the ceremony, Stephan invoked the Holy Archangel Michael and his heavenly army to defend me against the powers of darkness. I understood these powers of darkness were within my own being. I didn't want to hate the father of my children. I didn't want to be impatient with my mother when she questioned, "Why can't you find spiritual fulfillment in your Jewish tradition?" I knew that very few people understood that I had not gone looking for Gnosticism or for *any* religious affiliation. This path had come under my step; I had not been in the market for a mystical initiation in an ancient religion, one whose history is fraught with persecution and exile. I already had that with Judaism! I was not seeking a support network or a feel-good community. Exorcism, as I increasingly understood, was about liberating my soul from the dense complications of personality – the baggage of emotional and psychological diversions from my true soul's purpose. It was about spiritual Freedom.

Jesus, as I comprehend, is emblematic of a more perfect person, of freedom, of wild love – a realized being, eternally real in broader dimensions. I want to live in those dimensions, to allow life to balloon from this shell, this contraction where confusion and discord reign – this "Plato's Cave," where all is shadow and illusion. This dimension of attachment to financial strife, familial discord, and emotional torment is some kind of springboard to something greater, something free, all-loving, and harmonious – a heaven not above this world but an expansion of what is thought of as this world.

---

"The kingdom of heaven is spread across the world
and men do not see it."

GOSPEL OF THOMAS

---

The bishop places his right hand on my head and says: *"In the Name of Christ our indwelling Lord, I admit thee to the Order of*

*Exorcist...*" He hands me a sword, the symbol of spiritual will, and a book, the symbol of knowledge, "*...whereby thou shalt be strong in the warfare of the spirit.*"

Warfare symbolism is rife in the Judeo/Christian world, and I do not resonate with it. My focus is inward and attentive, listening to the voice of wisdom that for me is not about vanquishing an enemy but about following the light that makes its way through the darkness. It is that voice that brought me to Stephan. Mine is not a war but an uncovering, a remembering. The inner voice said: *Let this man guide you. Now at the millennium, in Los Angeles, where wisdom is scattered and vague, he will do.*

Stephan, however, was investing a lot of his intention in me. His church was a masculine form, and his dream was to have a powerful feminine figure at its center. He'd ordained women before but they'd all migrated away. He saw something in me that I didn't yet see myself. I was not aware that he was grooming me for that post.

Oh, men.

# Twin Angels

"It is time to waken him. The seer cannot be held to the eyes,
the being cannot be held to the body."

THE AVATARS BY Æ

Ali Akbar Khan's *Garden of Delight* is playing on the small stereo in the corner of Jan's bedroom, upstairs from the studio. Alone, I dance a twirling motion, my long wine-colored "beautiful-woman" dress spinning out like a dervish's over my nakedness. My marriage to David has openly ended, and Jan and I have been free to consummate our relationship.

Entheogen is a psychoactive substance used to generate the divine within. An hour ago, we took some "magic mushrooms" with this sacramental intention. Jan comes into the room and moves into my circle, taking the fabric of my dress into the lively confidence of his hands. He lifts my garment over my head and turns me into his embrace. We tumble to the bed under the red lumens of blessed quiet – the students are gone; his children have dispersed for the night.

Lying on his back, he rolls me on top of him. Feeling the dampness of my love for him, he rises to meet me. The magic mushrooms are beginning to quicken our perceptions and soften the borders between us. An opening channel makes our two hearts one and expands to spiritual brilliance, lifting us to the presence of light-filled love. We move inside the rhythms of Godlove, knowing it doesn't belong to us but we to it. Our sexuality is congruent with our spirituality, as deep and fluid as the oceans. My breathing intensifies to our waves and currents; it rushes in and out until breath is all I hear, surrounded by silence. And then even breath dissolves into timeless love…

Now, Jan gently taps on my lower back, calling me back to my body, to here-now awareness. "Shh," he whispers, "there is something here." I become quiet, alert to what he perceives. "It's enormous," he whispers reverently, "an angel…"

I remain still, attentive, and then I begin to see what I sense he is seeing – not with my eyes but with my visionary focus. This is not a hallucination or a trick of the mind but sight in a different sense, sight by means of spirit. A great masculine figure presents himself in this visionary field. He has huge wings, and a curving light emanates from him and around him. I feel a sense of blue – not the pigment but the vibration itself. Jan and I lay in each other's arms for a long time, rapt, as we witness this resplendent image. Eventually the vision wanes, but the resonance of its spiritual magnitude permeates our energy field; blessedness replaces normal sense perception. Jan slips out to go to the bathroom. I lie in the bed alone, still quivering from the visitation.

Then, like another wave gathering from the depths of eternity, I begin to hear music coming to my interior mind – a regal choir, formal and loud. I see a magnificent procession moving closer toward my visionary field. A queen stands high on a dazzling, square-stepped dais. She rolls toward me amid beautiful lights and colors. Her bearing is that of eminent dignity. I think, *the queen of heaven*. The procession moves inexorably closer to my vision, and now I can see her face. She is me. I see my own face, and I am filled with exaltation.

---

"I went and found my soul. What are to me all the worlds?
I went and found Truth, as she stands at the outer rim of the worlds."

GREAT BOOK OF THE MANDAEANS

---

The next morning, Jan and I have fried-egg sandwiches and coffee at Balthazar's café. I can feel how the resonance of our God-love experience the night before radiates out to others – the server, the deliveryman, the homeless woman, Balthazar himself – and how they reflect it back. It is an ordinary smoggy morning with impatient drivers honking car horns in the distance, and yet there is a different quality of smile on the people around us; they seem to echo the same spirit of kindness and gratitude that we are feeling. I see us as a pair of pink opalescent bubbles bringing joy and expansion to the people we encounter.

---

"Whoever has ears let him hear.
Within a man of light there is light, and he lights the whole world.
When he does not shine, there is darkness."

THE GOSPEL ACCORDING TO THOMAS

---

Newspapers are strewn about the tables for the patrons. I pick up the *Daily News*, February 20, 1993, and read the headline, "Mother Dies as Car Forced Off the Road." There's a picture of a two-year-old girl being carried by two firefighters to an ambulance. Their faces show immense compassion for the little girl, who is lying on a stretcher, stiffened by shock. Tears let loose down my cheeks as I struggle to contain the great divide of human experience in my one little heart. I am moving to the music of Oneness, of Godlove from my experience with Jan last night, and now – charging through the center of my symphony – is this little girl's tragedy. The shockwave reverberates in my soul. I feel it personally. I want to go to her and pour this eternal love into her life. I want to restore her to a deeper dimension, where her mother is not really gone but expanded to a greater reality.

∞

Later that evening, Jan and I talk quietly in the back studio, near where his icon painting of the Prophet Mani is set on an easel. I say, "I think we experienced our Twin Angels last night."[12]

Jan looks into me. His face shines, an unbroken sunny-side-up egg. "Yes," he says, "I think so."

[12] According to the prophet Mani, we each have a twin angel, a twin flame that is with Sophia – Wisdom.

# Big Dream: St. Francis

I am walking through the wide upper hallway of a medieval castle. The floor and walls are of heavy stone. I stop, remove all my jewelry, and place it in a small alcove to my right, then continue on. Ahead of me is an archway leading to the exterior. Walking steadily on, I can see the blue sky. Outside are two towerlike structures. They remind me of the towers in the Moon card of the Ryder Waite Tarot deck, which shows two arched windowlike openings at the top, the same shape as the alcove where I've left my jewelry. I continue walking straight off the floor. Now I am hung by my neck from one of the towers. I look down, way below to the ground. Many people are standing looking up at me aghast or turning away in sorrow and horror. I think, *they think what is happening to me is tragic, but they don't understand.* Just then St. Francis appears from the clouds. He takes me and wraps me in swaddling like a baby. Cradling me, he turns, and with me in his arms he returns to the Light.

---

Jesus said to John: Thou hearest of me suffering,
yet I have not suffered; pierced, yet was I not smitten; hanged,
but was not hanged; blood flowing from me, yet it did not flow.
And in a word, what they say of me, these things I did not have;
while what they do not say, those I have suffered. Understand me
then as the slaying of a Word, wound of a Word, hanging of a Word,
suffering of a Word, fastening of a Word, death of a Word,
resurrection of a Word, and defining this Word, I mean *every man!*

THE ACTS OF JOHN

---

# What Are We About?

Jan and I lie next to each other in the early dawn; pink-smog haze begins to lighten the room. What do we have here between us? Where is this going? I have experienced the dissolving spiritual love with "other" that I'd always championed, but he is leaving. He is always leaving. Not just back to Norway, as he has dreamed of doing ever since he was thrown by circumstance upon the Pacific shore, with its climate just too hot for his comfort, but also by his nature, like a fish, always swimming away, even as its opposite self swims toward. I don't feel a domestic life with him, and yet this closeness, this dissolving that we share, is something that I've always believed was possible – this love, this spirit living in the flesh, living between us, in our lovemaking, in our joining. Why would we leave this? What shall we do with this? Perhaps Jan is asking the same questions. He turns his gaze to me; oceans of love penetrate my soul through his powder-blue eyes. He whispers, "Hannah from Heaven." And then we drift into our personal reveries, toward the activities of the day.

Late that afternoon, after all the students have dispersed, I am alone with Jan in the studio. He comes toward me wiping his hands with his turpentine-scented rag. I put my brush down on my palette and step back from my easel. I sense him calling me toward a kind of hearing that requires my deep attention. He faces me, close, and speaks in a low, intimate tone: "The Christ spoke to me this morning." He pauses, waiting for me to settle my mind from its prior focus on my painting to hear his words. "The Christ spoke," he repeats. "He said, 'She belongs to me.' I cannot try to hold you as my own."

# CHAPTER 7

# Acolyte

# The Earth Moved

It is 4:40 a.m., January 17, 1994, and I'm propelled from sleep out of my bed to the bedroom doorjamb. The porch lights and street-lights crash off, and I'm surrounded by darkness. My wood-frame and plaster house roils and creaks. I hear glass crash to the floor. I sink down to a squat and become an animal frozen, waiting for the danger to pass, but the earthquake doesn't stop. The beams in the ceiling overhead and the floor beneath me keep slamming one way, then another. I'd be foolish to try to better my position because I can't see if anything is coming toward me. If I do so I could end up heading straight toward disaster. I just wait and bind myself to the doorframe, with the knowledge that somehow everything will be OK if I just wait. Something else breaks; more crashes; the house groans. Finally, there is quiet...then another rumble...then quiet.

I feel my way to the side of my bed. My sheepskin slippers are side by side exactly as I'd left them. I feel for the flashlight in the top drawer of my dresser, which has slid away from the wall. I get past the kitchen and am relieved to have found my slippers – the flashlight beam shows a floor covered with broken glass. In the service porch, the clothes dryer has slid in front of the back door. Thanks to this old house and its quirky structure, the door opens outward. I squeeze between dryer and wall to get outside.

The night sky has a Hades-red tinge, and I don't notice if there is a moon or what phase it is in. I hear nothing from the guest-house, where Dickon is sleeping with David, as I carefully tread the several yards between the houses, toward the bungalow's kitch-en door. Shock, worry, disorientation course through my body. I peer in through the kitchen-door window, shining my flashlight, and see the floor covered with broken dishes. I call out, *David...*

*Dickon*... Something is jammed against the door and I cannot open it (we never lock our doors). I call out again; still no answer. I begin to feel frantic. I bang on the back-bedroom door, no answer. Panic rises in my gut until finally David calls out, "We're OK" and opens the bedroom door. Another thunderous roar rises from deep underground, an aftershock. Straining his nonchalant British manner, David says, "It was just an earthquake; we're fine." His stiff-upper-lip imperturbability frustrates me.

I rush in to Dickon and pick him up, holding him so tight he has to wriggle out of my hold, "I'm fine mom. It was just an earthquake," he parrots his father. "Dad put a pillow over my head when the house was shaking. At first I thought he was trying to kill me," he laughs. David also gives a nervous laugh, the way he does when things are ultimately out of his control. I show him his own kitchen, trying to get some kind of response out of him. "Oh, my," he says with no exclamation, seeing how most of his dishes are shattered on the floor.

Sophia is sleeping over at her friend Rachel's house in Northridge. After seeing that Dickon and David are fine, I shakily rush back to my house where Rachel's phone number is still pinned to the bulletin board by the phone. Amazingly, there is a dial tone! Rachel's mother answers and assures me they are all unharmed. Just then the phone goes dead, and remains so for the next three days. I go back to the guesthouse. It feels unnatural for our family to be dispersed during a catastrophe like this. David wants to go back to sleep. "It's no big deal; we'll clean it up in the morning." There is no way I can go back to sleep; my body is shaking with adrenaline. I wish we'd had, at least now, some common sensibility. I find the emergency transistor radio on the floor and dial into a clear AM station. My body is still vibrating with anxiety.

Suddenly the ground begins to rumble again. "Whoa. We just experienced another aftershock," the radio announcer says, sounding shaken, comforting me with the knowledge that at least *someone* else acknowledges a major disturbance. I sit on the sofa listening to the news reports, learning that the earthquake is centered somewhere in Northridge, adjacent to Reseda, where we live. There are continuous aftershocks. Unlike the main house, built on a raised foundation, the guesthouse is built on a concrete slab and does not shake as violently.

David dozes in the bedroom through the aftershocks, while Dickon snuggles on the couch with me, listening, dozing, waiting, and riding the aftershocks until the blessed sun rises.

By 10 a.m., I decide to see what the roads look like and drive over to Rachel's house to pick up Sophia. The traffic lights are all out. There are few cars on the road, and drivers are cautious and respectful. Sirens ring all over the valley, and a few plumes of smoke rise from burning houses. Rachel's house looks normal; her mother shows me the damage in the kitchen and to the fireplace, but it isn't too bad. Sophia is packed up and ready to leave. The calamity doesn't seem nearly as devastating at Rachel's house as it is at ours. Then Sophia shows me a huge mahogany sideboard that toppled over into the center of the den. "We went to sleep last night in sleeping bags on the floor, right there," she points to where the cabinet now lays on its side. "But we decided to move to the couches cause the floor was too hard." A shudder runs up the center of my body and I grab Sophia into my arms and hold her with tears in my eyes, whispering, "Thank God, thank God."

My kitchen floor is rubble – olive oil, maple syrup, glass and ceramic shards. A wooden beam spears through the living-room ceiling; the brick chimney has fallen onto the roof. For three nights, the kids and I sleep in a tent in the backyard where the aftershocks become almost soothing since we know nothing can fall on us. The night sky is glorious. With the lights out through most of the city, the normally unseen heavens that surround us are visible.

Three weeks later, life began to return to order. The rhythm of the demise of our marriage resumed. King was over, and he and I sat on the back deck, drinking some Chardonnay. "Did you hear that they recalculated the epicenter of the earthquake to be right here, Wilbur and Saticoy, our exact corner?" I said.

King strummed his guitar and, turning his head from side to side, he sang, "Shake it up baby."

"I think it's time one of you move before you cause any more damage."

# Michael Returns

One Sunday in October, I arrived at church carrying my washed and pressed vestments, and I saw some ominous-looking ritual implements already set up on the red throne type chair reserved for special occasions: a black cape, a sword, and a skull. I realized it was the day commemorating the Martyrdom of the Knights Templar. I'd seen this celebration before but never felt any personal connection with it, and I knew better than to ask any questions about it. Stephan generally only discussed details with those who needed to know. It was his nature to be secretive. After all, the Gnosis survived for thousands of years by keeping its secrets below the radar of empires. All would be revealed in due time.

The bishop was vested in a red antique French alb. The Mass began as usual with five clergy. When it came time for the lesson, Jack-the-Bear handed me the book. By now I was confident at the altar, and I seamlessly took it from his hands and stepped forward to read the lesson to the congregation. I noticed Michael Lafferty sitting toward the back near the elegant gray-haired Jane, one of the congregants who came to this Gnostic church from a Theosophical background. Though it had been a year since Michael and I first met, and then only briefly, I felt a slight flutter of recognition: *he must be back from France.*

In the middle of the Mass the bishop invited Michael up to the altar. Stephan was performing a rare Templar ordination. Michael stepped confidently to the altar to be "knighted" in the Templar tradition, as Stephan had reconstructed it.

I felt no connection to this ceremony, nor to Knights Templar. Within the body of Gnosis, there are many forms, secret societies, sects, and mythologies. Bishop Steven Marshall describes it like this: "[This] might be symbolized in the image of an underground stream traveling through time and geography to surface and appear at various times in history. The Templars then are one such upwelling or surfacing of the Gnosis within the various and superficially dissimilar trappings of time and culture."

The underground streams that spoke to me were the ones with themes of acceptance and love, feminine qualities, and with Hermetic foundations. I did not resonate with the masculine warrior symbolism.

After the Mass, when candles were snuffed and clergy divested, I came out to greet Michael with a smile. I didn't know why but I already felt him to be a friend. It wasn't a sexual attraction; I just felt that I knew him and was at ease with him. We arranged to have lunch together at the Chinese restaurant in Los Feliz.

He orders moo-shu pork. "That's all I can eat so I'm not sharing," he says with a note of guilty petulance. We talk about France. "I have a house there, in the Dordogne, near a village called Belvès. Well, it's not actually my house but I restored it and decorated it for my friend Grace who is only there two weeks out of the year." He hands me a self-published book of poems. "This is what I've been doing. It's for you."

I am surprised that after a year and only meeting once or twice, he's brought me a gift. "Well, we're friends aren't we?" he says, almost with a pout, like a little child who would be hurt if I contradicted him. "I've traveled a lot in my life," he says. "I taught

English in Iran for a year; I was the top buyer for Gump's[13] and traveled all over for them. I went to France to die."

"Were you planning a suicide?" He didn't seem ill.

"I discovered I'm HIV positive and I assumed…I wanted to be in France when I went; it's very beautiful at the farmhouse. But I didn't die! I tended a garden and wrote poetry and became very lonely and not very sick, so I came back."

Soon, Michael entered the clergy, and we moved congruently up the initiatory ladder.

---

Receive the mysteries of the Light in this afflicted time, and go into
the kingdom of the Light. Do not add day to day or cycle to cycle,
hoping to come to receive the mysteries when we come to the world
in another cycle. Now such people do not know when the number of
the Perfect Souls will be complete, and I shall shut the
Gates of Light, and from that time no one shall go in,
because the mystery of the first mystery has been accomplished,
for whose sake the universe has come into being.

THE BOOK OF SOPHIA

---

# Topanga Refuge

---

"My heart was pruned and its flower appeared,
then grace sprang up in it."

THE ODES OF SOLOMON

---

[13]A large decorating firm in San Francisco

I took King's little song advice to heart and began to look for a house to rent in Topanga Canyon, where Kristine lived. I saw an ad for a rental – "by seasonal stream, under live oaks." It turned out to be no more than a trailer behind an empty lot where the old *Country Club*, a rock 'n' roll club from the sixties, had been torn down. The "seasonal stream" was really just a wash. I imagined pairing my life down to poverty, sitting on the metal stoop of the trailer with Dickon sleeping in the bunk while Sophia and I did handicrafts at a picnic table under the trees – happy hippy peasants living a simple, back-to-nature life in the woods. Meanwhile Sophia was already resisting the idea of moving.

"You are not living here, Hannah." Kristine was adamant. "It's too small. And the creek will rise and you won't be able to get out. Sophia won't even visit you." I knew she was right. I really did want to simplify my life, but I was so depleted and demeaned by the dynamic of my marriage and its unraveling that I couldn't discern between simplicity and self-denigration.

"I see you up on Cheney," Kristine said. The following week she found a notice for a house for rent on Callon Drive. We looked at a map and saw that Callon is in the Cheney area. Kristine is a genie for finding the right home, for both herself and her friends. The minute we walked into the empty house, Kristine saw the black-and-white floor tiles in the hallway, and said, "This is your house." Her paintings at the time all featured those same black-and-white tiles. I was not sure. There were only two bedrooms.

"I'm not moving, Mom," Sophia insists. She is sullen and resistant. She is now fourteen, and lawyers have counseled that she has the right to choose which parent she lives with.

"Just look at it," I plead. I drive her up to Topanga, hoping the hills and nature will speak to her. We walk through the empty house together. "You can have the big bedroom. I'll sleep in the living room." I try to help her visualize a life here, surrounded by oak trees.

Topanga is a rural area in the Santa Monica Mountains. It has a rare mix of small-town rural life surrounded by the cities of Los Angeles County. I imagine her making friends with some of the local teens and maybe getting into riding horses; perhaps she'll get involved with the Theatricum Botanicum, an outdoor theater founded by Will Geer, which has classes and events for teens.

"I'm not moving. Can we go?"

As we drive back down to the valley, I feel a great weight pulling my daughter down, down, down, like Persephone being abducted by Hades. My guts are being wrenched and my heart is wailing in my chest. I pull the car over and put my hands on her shoulders. Tears stream down my cheeks as I look into her eyes and say, "Whatever happens, I promise, I won't let go of you." I want her to know that even though I can't make her come with me, I will always be here when she wants to come back to me. She chooses to live with her dad.

In February of 1994, Dickon and I moved to the Callon house. Michael and other friends from the Gnostic Society came to help. I rented a U-Haul truck, which we loaded and drove to the new house. I took only what I loved and needed to live simply. The day was sunny, and spring was all around as we caravaned over to the new house.

The restored gold-mining cabin was spotlessly clean. All along the side of the house, jasmine was in bloom, and the scent made me feel like I was moving into heaven. A beautiful front deck overlooked the small street. Single women lived in each of the three houses around us – to our left, right, and across the street. There was a little girl Dickon's age across the street, and they became friends. It was the perfect house to live the simple St. Francis life that I wanted. Dickon and I each had our own bedroom. He lived with me during the week and went to David's on the weekends.

# Orb Vision Affirms Life

Jan had been in Oslo for a month. I had a dream that became a powerful waking vision: I walk over to the Thai restaurant near Bruchion to look for Jan. I see him there through the window, and when I go inside it is some sort of esoteric library. He is sitting at a table engrossed, studying with books spread out around him. He is wearing some kind of listening or translating device around his head. It reminds me of the tefillin that religious Jewish men wear around their heads – leather straps with little leather boxes packed with prayers that sit on the front of the head above the third eye. I go up to him and ask how long he will be. He looks into my eyes and says, "I have to stay here now." I leave.

I wake from the dream into a state of profound aloneness. I know the dream is telling me my time with Jan is really over now. He has come and gone between Norway and L.A. several times since we've been "together," and I've gotten used to time without him. But now he will return to L.A. before moving permanently back to his homeland. I've always known this time would come. Jan has said from the beginning that he plans to return to Norway. But like the certain knowledge that death will come to everyone, when you lose someone so permanently, it sucks out your insides and leaves you without bones.

Still in bed, I lay on my back like a corpse with my arms at my side. The grief of this existential barrenness presses down on me. The weight of it is so heavy, I can't even panic or attempt to escape it. Contracted into my own soul with Jan whirling away from the sharing of it, I have no place to run, no avenue of evasion. I've been practicing "surrender" since I began this journey. My marriage is a train wreck, my daughter refuses to have anything to do with me, and now this separation. Even this I must accept – this black hole where no "friend" is. I remain alert. I cannot flee into sleep. This acceptance requires my presence. I let myself go into the void…

At the moment of complete acceptance I feel a rising up coming from below me, like an enormous orb lifting me. My bed disappears and now I am adhered to this sphere, a new foundation. There is no down or up, but like a planet in space it takes its place in the void. I am like a caryatid fused to the sphere, looking out to the cosmos. I myself become a window through which light from the orb shines, emanating outward to humanity. And then I realize I am not alone – there are others also fixed to this globe in various places around the sphere, also windows through which light from the sphere projects outward – Jan, Stephan, and many more.

Now I feel exultant. The sublime cosmic sound of joy is harmonic everywhere. The turning from darkest desolation to most meaningful purpose of life is instantaneous, pivoting on the pinpoint of complete acceptance.

# Attire as Personal Vestments

David let Sophia live in the guesthouse on her own. I cried and worried about her constantly, helpless to do anything about her living condition. I felt she'd been abandoned to the back of the property, rarely having meals with her father or spending much time with him at all. She never wanted to see me. I tried to catch glimpses of her when I took Dickon to school, and I seized impromptu moments to speak with her teachers about how she was doing.

For some reason the maid never cleaned the guesthouse, and it became horribly dirty, with cobwebs that some of Sophia's friends thought were leftover Halloween decorations. One day while she was at school and David at work, I went over there to clean. I stripped the bed, washed her sheets and towels, and vacuumed and dusted. A mound of discarded clothing was crumpled on the floor of the closet. I took it all out and sorted through it. In the pile was a little yellow sleeveless rayon top, cut in an A shape. I liked it and took it home with me.

When I was married, David bought me lovely clothes. Now my clothing was beginning to turn drab. All the elastic in those Laise Adzer skirts and pants that Bobbie and Laurel so admired had lost their elasticity. I needed a new look, but I hated shopping and never liked spending money on myself or working on my wardrobe. My favorite thing to put on in the morning was what I'd worn the day before, if it wasn't dirty. I figured if it was good yesterday it would be fine today. I had a list of prerequisites for a functional wardrobe. I wanted attire that was as appropriate for a teacher conference or churchgoing as for a walk in the hills above my cabin. They had to be comfortable and versatile. That little yellow rayon top inspired a core design based on the triangle. By simply lengthening the triangle of that top, I made dresses that flowed, could be tied up at the hems for hiking, and dressed up or down, depending on the occasion. Under those garments, my body felt as comfortable as being naked. They were as unrestrictive as pajamas. They concealed everything about my body and yet I felt and looked sexy, in a goddessy, priestessy sort of way. They were like street-wear vestments, like the desert garments of the land where I was born, and they became my entire wardrobe.

# Ordination to Acolyte

*"Beloved daughter, you are about to be admitted to the order of acolyte, which is the most advanced of the grades of the lesser mysteries in the Ecclesia of the Gnosis.*

"Will you ever serve faithfully before the altar of your heart, and offer upon it your life as a sacrifice to Divinity?"

"I will." The word sacrifice, rooted in the word sacred, is taking deeper significance for me. All I have sacrificed, including mothering my own daughter, is forging the altar of my heart.

"As you are now admitted to this order, wherein you come within the very orbit of the central and most holy mystery of the Gnosis, I must admonish you never to forget that you now draw nigh not to an earthly altar, but to that most sacred and inmost center of your self. Such is the life of the divine ones; a life that has no attachment to earthly things, a flight of the alone to the Alone."

The orbit I have circled with Jan is now spiraling me toward a dimension more mysterious and remote. I do not resist the heartache or try to cover it up with drink or drugs or distractions. Jan and I have been each other's initiators. Although he is already an ordained priest, there are deeper mysteries of holy presence that we've shared. "Love is a cold and a broken Hallelujah."[14]

One evening several months earlier, I arrived at Bruchion where Jan, Charles, and Kristine were about to open a bottle of wine. "We need an opener," Charles said, just as I entered the room. Jan extended his arm toward me with a smile, saying, "Here is my opener." Jan and I had danced together around an indefinable mystic light. That dance positioned me to more deeply fulfill my childhood vision. I believe it gave him what he needed then also.

"O Christ, our inmost and mystic central Sun, around whom the holy dance of all luminaries ceaselessly revolves, thou flame whose scattered sparks we are, thou Lord of the center of all circles, seer of all entrances and partings ... In the Name of Christ our indwelling Lord, I admit thee to the Order of Acolyte."

---

[14] Leonard Cohen

# Presence in the Chapel

In September of 1994, Jan moved permanently to Oslo. That October, Kristine moved to New Mexico. I felt friendless and alone. An arid spiritualism dropped into my soul and displaced the sexy, feisty spiritus that had called me onto this initiatory path. But I'd committed myself to this process and I'd responded to a true voice within me. I knew from what I'd learned about spiritual journeys that this barrenness, this aloneness when all your friends are gone, is part of the deal. I was truly living in the state of being that the ritual ordination to acolyte had placed me in – *"to serve faithfully before the altar of my heart, and offer upon it my life as a sacrifice to Divinity." I had taken the "flight of the alone to the Alone,"* remembering my childhood experience of crying on the lawn in deep sorrow. I recognized that within the word alone sits "All One" where I and Thou are the same being.

In the calm acceptance of what is, knowing there was no place else for me to be, nowhere to run, I reiterated in a deeply personal and private voice, this sacrifice of myself to the divine teacher within, that which had brought me to this loneliness. *Beloved Christ of my soul, I give myself to you. You are the only one who gives me life; it is the life of your life that I long for.*

On Tuesday mornings Stephan said Mass privately in a small chapel in the Hollywood Hills, surrounded by pine trees. The Tuesday after I made my private sacrifice to the Christ within, I assisted Stephan with this Mass.

At the first censing I begin to feel something inordinately transcendent. Everything in the room and in me becomes wavy, the way air looks around a hot fire. I am transported into a stained-glass dimension of light that dazzles more than my eyes. My skin loses its sense of boundary, and I am not separate from but made of the magneto energy that infuses all of life. This is akin to the visions spoken of by mystics, where the seer is overcome by what feels like a visitation from God. Tears flood down my cheeks, and my mind and senses are so altered that when Stephan hands me the lectionary to read the lesson, I'm not sure I even *can* read. I am inside love-kaleidoscopic and can barely focus my eyes on the page.

This shift into this other dimension came not at the consecration – the part of the ritual when the Christ, who is an other-dimensional being, is invited in – but of its own immense will, independent of the structure of the Mass. It was as if two occurrences happened simultaneously: the shift into another dimension, and the performance of the Eucharist. But these two did not seem to occur by cause and effect. By the time the consecration actually took place, the feelings had subsided, and I was left with images of large abstract movements of brilliant, complex deep color, irreverently drifting outside the lines that define forms. Later I conceded that I might not have had the experience had I not been participating in the Eucharist.

The Mass came to its completion, and we divested as if no extraordinary cosmic occurrence had just taken place. Stephan waited expectantly for me to say something; he recognized that *something* had occurred for me. But I didn't have the vocabulary for what had just happened. The only words that came to mind – words like "the Christ came to me," words like "rapture" – sounded so mundane, so cliché, so fundamentalist, compared to the experience, that I dared not speak them.

# CHAPTER 8

# Subdeacon

# Only Love

On December 28, 1994, Jan telephones from Oslo. His friend Qvell has hung on to life all these months and is now approaching his death – he is in a partial coma. "He goes in and out of consciousness," Jan says, with sorrow and acceptance. "He told me yesterday when he was present that he is traveling through many mysteries and that I am always there with him. He said that coming back to his body is like sucking wide open space into an excruciating contraction." Jan is silent for a moment. We listen together to the long-distance hum of the telephone. Punctuating the stream of thought that has gone unspoken, he talks about how certain characteristics his friend bore used to disturb him. Then he says, "What we thought were his weaknesses turned out to be his strengths." We are silent again as that thought sinks in. He speaks again, "tonight, just before he went back into the coma, he looked deeply into my eyes. He said, 'Jan you must always remember: only love and the acts of love matter.'"

Eventually we say good-bye and I hang up the phone. I sit there in my Topanga cabin; golden light from the candles dances on the auburn wood paneling. After so many years of self-examination and therapy, I am an expert on all of my weaknesses. I can even admit them to a few close friends. Now I sit and simply imagine each one of these known weaknesses as strength. I turn each one of them inside out: Where I am hesitant to speak up, I see that I am able to keep my own council. Where I sometimes become frustrated and lose my temper, I see a desire for greater balance. Where I have wasted my affections indiscriminately, I see my capacity to love. As I continue to turn the coins of these weaknesses over, a quiet grace fills my heart, the grace of self-forgiveness. I contemplate the word "forgiveness." Fore-given – it is a given that being human is inconsistent, imperfect. Spiritual weakness is woven into the fabric of every human being's "mingled nature, the sleep of this world." How foolish then to not accept this actuality – to judge, to condemn the very thread that makes the fabric what it is. To forgive, then, is not to condone or to grant absolution but to accept the nature of being human.

# Leap to a Higher Order

I recognize that the next initiatory phase is not a step but rather a leap to the higher orders, which begins with Subdeacon. By now, the ordinations are coming naturally to me, and I am certain that I will persist to the priesthood. I am as a mountain climber who had initially set out on an exploratory hike at the base of a mountain. As the trail narrows, the air becomes thinner, the weather colder. This ordination is like being given the tools I need to reach the summit: the ropes, the crampons and pitons, the bivy sacks.

On April 30, 1995, I stand before the bishop, who is vested in white, as he incants the Collect, *"O unseen God ... Arouse her soul from the sleep of this world and awaken her to the mysteries no rulership and no authority, no subject nor mingled nature can understand ..."*

Now I confidently listen to the "unstruck sounds and what sifts through that music," as in the Rumi poem that confirmed my praying mantis experience.

The bishop, now seated on his faldstool, holds his brass crosier as he continues with the ordination, *"Beloved Daughter, you are about to be admitted to the office of Subdeacon, which is the first of the greater mysteries in the Ecclesia of the Gnosis ... It gives those who receive it greater strength and steadfastness of purpose, to the end that, with singleness of heart, they may dedicate their lives to the Gnosis of God ... not doubting that at the latter end, you, as a faithful ministrant of the mysteries, will receive from on high the robe of glory, the golden garment of the Gnosis of God."*

My personal odyssey with the *Hymn of the Pearl* continues:

---

And I snatched away the pearl,
and turned to go back to my father's house.
And their filthy and unclean dress I stripped off,
and left it in their country;
and I took my way straight to come
to the light of our home in the East.
And my letter, my awakener,
I found before me on the road;
and as with its voice it had awakened me,
[so] too with its light it was leading me."

HYMN OF THE PEARL

---

The ritual ceremonies at the higher levels of ordination are more extensive and more formal. I lie prostrate on the floor with my head toward the bishop, my arms outstretched. The congregation kneels, hands together in prayer mudra, and chants the litany. I breathe in the aromatic frankincense and feel a great good will coming from all of the congregants and clergy, like sunshine and warmth.

Standing again, facing the bishop, he continues describing the symbolic significance of the various pieces of vestments, *"...Those who enter this Order ... strive to acquire certain virtues of character ... By the amice, control of speech; by the maniple, the love of service, of diligence in all good works; by the tunicle, the spirit of joy and gladness, freedom from care and depression, that is to say, confidence... [in divinity]." Will you then strive, as far as in you lies, to order your life in accordance with these precepts?*

"I will."

Jack-the-Bear hands me the lectionary to read the lesson for the Mass, taken from the Hermetic Revelation of the Nine by the Eight:

"... *Grant us to see, through Spirit, the form of the image, which has no flaw ... For it is through Thee that the all received animation ... Make whole that which is within us, and grant us the wisdom of the immortal ones!*"

This ordination ceremony speaks of the responsibilities of the office and of service as it pertains to church activity. It also speaks of "growing in knowledge of things eternal."

It was not enough for me to have mystical experiences, however stunning they were. I was now gaining strength through this ordination to be steadfast in spirit, regardless of whether I tasted the frosting or just the crumbs of the spiritual cake. There is a teaching in wisdom traditions of the wheel. The challenge is to move along the spokes of the wheel to the center, where the context of the outer rim of the wheel is not so influential. The outer rim circles up and down, and if you are stuck on the outer rim, it tosses you round and round with it. When it is up off the ground, you are joyful, elated, and feel free, because of happy circumstance. When it is down you are depressed and feel crushed, beaten, downhearted, and crestfallen. The subdeaconate is designed to assist you in furthering your efforts toward the center of the wheel, where you are not tossed about by moods and events. It takes diligence and dedication, daily practice and constant reiteration of your goal, because the distractions are infinite – what Lao Tsu calls The Ten Thousand Things. For me the straw dogs of distraction often wear the cloak of meaningful intent. I could spend twenty-five hours a day on efforts to improve the environment, bring sanity to politicians, feed the hungry, save the whales, fight Monsanto. I am very happy that there are people who make these efforts. But my soul's purpose is called to a different task—to puncture the bubble of delusion; like Frodo in *The Lord of the Rings*, to destroy the ring of power, within myself and for the sake of all mankind.

*Here endeth the lesson.*

# When the Student Is Ready, the Teacher Comes

---

"On a sudden, when I received it,
the garment seemed to me to become like a mirror of myself."

HYMN OF THE PEARL

---

There was a man I'd seen in Gnostic Society circles for years. His name was Roger Weir, and I didn't know much about him other than he was a friend of both Stephan and Jan. He had owned a bookstore on Hollywood Boulevard some years back, and David had been to his shop several times in the early days when we were just back from England. Roger had sold Jan his old Mercedes, which Jan had restored through trades with the neighboring auto mechanic/ body shop.

Stephan lectured every Friday night at the Gnostic Society, speaking on topics such as Jungian interpretations, Tarot, Gnostic Gospels, and Hermeticism. One Friday evening, in the autumn of 1994, Roger was scheduled to substitute for Stephan who would be out of town on a lecture tour. Elegant Jane said to me, with a glow in her eyes, "Oh, he's a marvelous speaker." Jane was a longtime friend of Stephan's who'd been involved with many of the well-known Theosophists and Spiritualists. Most of the clergy were out of town or otherwise engaged and unable to attend that Friday night, so I took it upon myself to attend Roger Weir's talk, both out of my own interest, to experience this speaker who had been in the periphery of my world, and also to unlock the door, make the coffee, and be responsible for the money.

Roger begins his talk by saying it is hard to speak wisdom in this age. Language and minds have been so corrupted and distanced from true wisdom that they are unable to even recognize it, much less hear it. He speaks of the ancient wisdom ability to use language that goes directly to the mind without getting caught in the ears. He explains that the Sanskrit version of that is "mantra," and the Egyptian form is called Hieroglyphic—"a language that would register deep enough in the mind that its focus would come to manifestation after death," he said.

As Roger speaks I experience what he speaks of. The mind in my head comprehends his words, and also the mind in my heart and whole being feels *Presence* coming directly into me from his words. I feel in some mysterious way deeply recognized, and it brings a thrill to my whole being.

After his talk, when people were milling about drinking coffee and eating cookies, I overheard him tell someone that he spoke regularly from his home in Silverlake on Saturday mornings at 10 a.m. He extended an open invitation. He said the address, and it seemed to register in my mind in that same place of wisdom he'd been speaking to in his talk; I remembered it.

The following Saturday morning, I had to drive downtown to Union Train Station to pick up Sophia. She was returning by train from a school trip to the Southwest. Silverlake was on our way home, and Sophia waited in the car while I ran in to give Roger the money he'd collected from the night before. Pushing through a plain wooden gate from the sidewalk, I faced a long stairway that ascended up through a garden hillside of hanging vines and lush jungled flora. The house was a small wooden bungalow filled with books, floor to ceiling on every wall, including the kitchen. People were milling about waiting for the talk to begin. I felt I'd entered a wisdom school, like some sort of glass-bead game, both ancient and timeless.

Roger invited me to stay for the talk but I told him I'd have to come back next week as my teenage daughter was waiting in the car, tired from a long journey. I didn't realize he knew Sophia. Some time later, she came with me to one of his talks. He told her that he'd been to her baptism at the Gnostic Church and that it was the only baptism he'd ever been to. She said it was probably the only one she'd ever been to also. He responded with an open heart, "That means we share something special." I didn't remember him attending her baptism; he never invested much of his time in church ceremonies.

The following Saturday, I return to Roger's home to attend the class. From behind an antique mahogany desk, and before a large Jeffersonian arched window of beveled panes, Roger Weir delivers his talks. He speaks of Inanna, the epic death and resurrection myth written by the daughter of Sargon of Akkad 4,000 years ago. I have been reading a book called *Descent to the Goddess*[15]. It is a Jungian psychological exploration of the Inanna story that the marriage counselor, whom David and I had seen during the demise of our marriage, had recommended I read. She felt this story resonated with what I was experiencing. Inanna divests herself of her jewels and garments and goes down into the underworld to greet her dark sister, Ereshkigal. She is hung on a hook and dies, but is rescued and resurrected to life by Enki, the water king.

I have a strong sense while listening to Roger that I am being shepherded toward deeper wisdom, and I feel less alone. Here is a guide, exactly where I am wandering. I have a bumper sticker on my car that says, "Not all who wander are lost." Here, with the teachings of Roger Weir, I feel deeply found.

Woven into Roger's extemporaneous presentation, he explains this is not just an independent lecture on a given subject but a two-year course delivered every Saturday. "If I could do this in a weekend workshop, I would. But it takes time to learn to hear wisdom," he says. I feel no hesitation—*I'm in*. My whole being vibrates harmoniously to *YES*.

Roger's wife told me later that of the twenty or so people who had attended the lecture on that Friday night at the Gnostic Society, I was the only person who came to attend Roger's course, though he'd extended the invitation to all. *When the student is ready, the teacher will come, and those who have ears will hear.*

When Stephan returned from his lecture tour, I mentioned to him that I'd been to Roger's lecture that Friday night at the Gnostic Society. His response was jolly. "Oh yes, he's a great speaker." But weeks later, as we were vesting for Mass in the tiny vestry, I detected a slight air of foreboding in Stephan's response when I mentioned I was now regularly attending Roger's talks on Saturdays.

[15] *Descent to the Goddess: A Way of Initiation for Women*, by Sylvia Brinton Perera

# CHAPTER 9

# Deacon

# Ordination to Deacon

In the Pythagorean Wisdom Schools, the beginners were known as *acousmatiques* – the listeners. For five years they were not allowed to speak, only to listen. It was understood that beginners didn't know enough to even ask the right questions. I am deepening my capacity to listen from silence, to silence, by hearing the wisdom teaching of Roger Weir each week.

I moved in my world now like a modern *acousmatique*. My role and responsibilities as mother took weekends off, because Dickon was with David on the weekends. On Saturday mornings I would rise, appreciating my solitude, dress, and drive down the hill to the Ventura Freeway heading east. Where the 101 freeway split off to the right toward Hollywood, I'd take the 134 freeway left to Silverlake for Roger Weir's class. On Sunday mornings I'd take the 101 toward Hollywood for the Gnostic Eucharist.

I was finally faithfully adhering to that inner voice, which as a child told me *try to live as much like Jesus Christ as you can.* Bishop Stephan Hoeller's staunch ritual forms and Roger Weir's wisdom teaching became two pillars of stability for me, two prongs of a tuning fork. I was the instrument being tuned. What was growing in me, in the space between these two pillars of learning, was a real *Person.* Not a *persona*, not a jumble of neurotic reactions, but some One.

---

"Not until we know the Self as One
can we overcome our addictive attachments to worldly things
and truly enjoy what we possess on Earth."

BISHOP STEVEN MARSHALL

---

I'd given up my art studio when I gave up the house to David and moved to the small cabin in Topanga Canyon. Our cabin had no garage in which to get messy with clay or paint. My parents gave me their old computer, a glorified word processor, and I learned to play around with it. Poetry began to erupt from me. For so long I'd lacked trust in my talents. It was a long journey toward comprehending my very real need to create. Now I experienced the creative process unencumbered. In the studio, I was always looking for pliers, lugging boxes of clay, setting up a palette, or cleaning up dried paint. Writing suited my nature because it was clean and unencumbered. When words or thoughts came to me, I could put them down in the midst of making dinner for Dickon and myself, or doing other household chores. I didn't need to change my clothes or carve out whole blocks of time in the studio – "In the beginning *is* the word."

∞

On May 26, 1996, Pentecost, the day that commemorates the Holy Spirit blowing into the soul so that all languages, all differences, are acknowledged and accepted, and oneness among peoples is experienced, I am ordained a Deacon of the Gnostic Ecclesia.

"*...Help thy chosen one this day and lift her soul above the weary phantoms of this world ... that she may breathe freely, repose in thy love, be at rest and return, arrayed with thy robe of glory, to do and bear whatever thou shalt ordain for her on the path of her sacred office...*"

How was Stephan to know that "*whatever thou shalt ordain*" might not be what he himself wanted? I came to this Gnostic initiation in response to the truest voice I'd ever known, the voice of my own life. This voice became clearer and clearer as I progressed through the ancient initiation that Stephan had reestablished in modern times – the church he so steadfastly and lovingly built. I knew this voice, above all others, was the guidance I must follow. Not my parents' or teachers', not David's or Stephan's or Jan's voices ever resounded as truthfully as the voice of my own life. I referred to this voice as *the Christ within*, though its name is less relevant than its quality. It came to me through the rituals and myths; it also came through a passing stranger or a dream. It didn't speak as a singular voice of authority but as a paired expression – my current challenges being met by Something Other, on the resonant wave of Wisdom.

Now, a fully ordained Deacon, I stood before the congregation fully vested as a reverend – a Deacon is considered reverend – minus the collar. I had not thought to add that item to my clerical wardrobe.

"The Gospel is taken from the *Gospel of Saint Thomas*"

*Jesus said: "What you will hear in your ear, in the other ear proclaim from your rooftops. For no one lights a lamp and puts it under a basket, nor does one put it in a hidden place. Rather, one puts it on a stand so that all who come and go will see its light."*

I did not know yet that the Gnostic Church might not be the rooftop from which I was to proclaim my light.

*Here endeth the Gospel.*

# CHAPTER 10

# Priest

# Listening Toward the Priesthood

In January 1998, I met with Stephan at his upstairs apartment in the Hollywood foothills and confessed, "I'm ready." He knew exactly what I meant. I sat on the couch, which was a sofa bed, across from him. He sat on a cushioned chair with wooden arms, a sword with a Templar standard hanging from it, positioned behind him. We sipped strong Turkish coffee from porcelain demitasses. He was dressed in a suit and leather shoes, with a red cravat round his neck. His apartment walls were lined with bookshelves of esoteric books, with a few Stephen King novels. We set the date for my ordination to the priesthood for March 15, the Ides of March. I thought that being ordained on the date of Julius Caesar's demise was apropos. I had always believed in personal freedom and had no desire to render anything more of myself to empire.

Michael's initiation had surged through the early stages, and he and I now moved through the ranks, parallel to each other. He was also ready for his ordination. He was like the "energizer bunny." He suffered his illness, took a lot of medication, and complained to anyone who would listen – but he never gave up. His motto was "*fortis in adversis*," fortitude in adversity. Believing very much in the hierarchical structure, he felt a little awkward finally setting his date, because it turned out to be three weeks before mine and he always thought of me as senior to him. "I couldn't care less dear," I reassured him. "However it works out. Your ordination is yours, and my ordination is mine."

Michael came to my house often so we could rehearse the Mass together. We each made and decorated our own copies of the Mass book. He made his with a traditional brocade fabric covering. I put images of St. Francis and a Buddha's hand in the teaching mudra on mine. I created electronic files with the rubrics (symbolic instructions about kneeling, moving to the left or right, and so on) that we would need: one set for the ordination itself and one for the Mass that we'd be celebrating.

Michael ordered a tall ornate gold-plated chalice with a wide base from a church-supply catalog. I deliberated for several weeks about my chalice. We looked through his catalogs and walked around the display cases at Cotters Church Supply, discussing the various possibilities. I'd seen an image in a book of the Antioch Chalice, which is presently in the Metropolitan Museum of Art, in New York, and I wished for at least a replica of it. It is thought to be the actual Holy Grail of the Last Supper and the image of it has a resonance for me of something very powerful and holy. No other chalices that Michael and I looked at came close to emanating the spirit of the Antioch Chalice. Unfortunately there was no replica, and in the end I bought a simple, inexpensive chalice for which I had no particular feeling. I was not very enthusiastic about acquiring any of the accoutrements that accompany the priesthood, and I subconsciously resisted the white priest collar in particular. Stephan said, "You can wait for that. It's not necessary yet," and I kept neglecting to put it on my list of things I needed.

∞

Lance was a Gnostic priest who lived in Salt Lake City and came to our congregation as a visiting priest every few months. He was from the Mormon tradition, a doctor, a mountain climber, and a scholar of C.G. Jung. Several years earlier, we'd become close friends and would often lunch together after Mass at the Chinese restaurant when he was in town. He made a point of planning one of his trips to coincide with my ordination, and he came bearing a gift for me: a beautiful white silk French chasuble. Another clergy member found a silk stole for me that happened to match. Jan timed a visit to

Los Angeles to correspond with my ordination, and Lance, Jan, and I spent the eve of my event together in quiet preparation.

That Sunday morning, the church was abuzz with restrained enthusiasm. There were more people in the congregation than on ordinary Sundays. Though women were openly accepted in the clergy, the ordination to Priesthood of a woman was a little less common. King was the only friend from my old "Ethel" life who came to witness my event.

The ordination begins with the Bishop reading the Collect, *"...Pour forth thy sanctifying grace into the heart of thy daughter who is about to be numbered among the Priests of thy holy mysteries."*

Jan reads the lesson from the Prophet Mani, *"O Servant of God...thou hast been called; do not fail to hear. Look back no more, they do not keep account of what is past, so do not think of what thou hast forgetfully done. Strain thyself forward and God will not turn thee away ...If thou hast resolved to love Me, then I will put on thee the robe of glory and the garland of victory, because thou hast believed in the truth..."*

Jan stands by me and formally presents me to the Bishop.

*"Wilt thou ever be mindful that in this priestly office to which thou art called it is thy duty to serve the Gnosis of the most high God, and not the works of an exoteric church?"*

"I will."

I'm not thinking just then that even this little storefront church might be "exoteric."

The bishop invokes the *"olden and awesome names, which men know not"* and performs the Litany with me prostrate before him.

*"...May wisdom guide and direct her life..."*

The bishop places his hands on my head, then all the priests who are present successively follow suit. Eight men of the Gnostic mystery, seven priests and one bishop, extend their energy to me. Lance had said of his own ordination, "I saw hands behind hands behind hands, generations of the carriers of the mystery, all the way back to Jesus."

The bishop stands up from his faldstool, takes the stole that hangs over my left shoulder and places it on my right shoulder, crossing it over my breast. *"Take thou this stole, for a symbol of the power of the priestly office and as a channel of the ever-flowing stream of Christ's love."* Lance and Jan place the chasuble over my head, and then the bishop anoints my hands with oil and breathes over them, whispering a holy name. I stand face to face with the bishop, and he solemnly says, *"THOU ART A PRIEST FOREVER, ACCORDING TO THE ORDER OF MELCHIZEDEK!"*

Stephan and I now move behind the altar; side-by-side, facing the congregation, we resume celebrating the Eucharist together. I read, "The Gospel is taken from the Gospel according to Saint Thomas."

*"Jesus said: If they say to you: 'From where have you originated,' you say to them: 'We have come from the Light, where the Light has originated through itself'..."*

I suddenly recall the dream I'd had of my origins – the crystalline cavern full of dazzling light that reminded me of the Superman movie. It was the dream that showed me how different David and I really were.

We arrive at the consecration. Stephan is an old soldier at the altar and has experienced many slips and unusual occurrences. "You must always read the Missal," he counsels. "Even though you know the words, the spiritual fire up there at the altar can sometimes throw you off." As he lifts his chalice to his lips I notice a wave of disorientation pass over him. The chalice slips slightly and spills red port on the white linen. He lets it pass and continues on.

The bishop and I complete the Eucharist together; I synchronize my speech to his rhythm, reciting the words that I both read and know from memory. I feel uncannily at ease with myself sharing the altar with this man who previously, in my incarnation as Ethel, had intimidated me by his knowledge and presence. We conclude with only a little extra pomp; the words of the Mass are not any different than on normal Sundays. We return to the vestry but do not divest; first we need to pose for photographs.

In front of the church, there is a festive feeling among the congregants. Cameras click and many people congratulate me with wide smiles. Lance leans toward Stephan and smiles ironically, whispering something about Stephan spilling the wine at the consecration. Sotto voce, Lance says, "She is a dissolver of all things," implying that it was I who caused Stephan's disorientation.

Are we not aiming to be dissolvers of all things? The Post-Eucharistic Prayer says: *"For inasmuch as we dissolve the world and are not dissolved ourselves, we are Lords of all creation and destruction."* I believe this is akin to making our way to the center of the wheel, rather than being tossed about on the rim, for in the center we are no longer subject to the whims of the world but are creators of our own destiny.

My old friend King cuts through the vested crowd and throws his arms around me. Ever the clown, he smiles and says, "Father Hannah." Ironically, though Gnosis always included women, the language of gender does not come into it. A woman priest in Stephan's church is not called "priestess." The mystery of my new position unfolds and I have a whimsical recognition. Since I'd renounced academia, I never imagined I'd have letters attached to my name, but now I possessed a prefix: Rev.

# Vipassana and Magdalene

In the beginning of July, four months after my ordination, I attend a Vipassana meditation training in Northern California taught by S.N. Goenka. The ten-day course is spent in silence, meditating ten hours a day. Though I've cavalierly signed up for the course, I am unsure if I can really do it, but I'm willing to try. My first Mass is scheduled for the end of July on the Festival of Mary Magdalene, and I intuitively feel that silence is the best way to prepare.

I am one of the first to arrive at the meditation center in a pastoral locale near Yosemite. The volunteer trainers give me my assigned cabin and cot number, and show me where the women's side is – men and women have separate lodgings. I find the cabin and, immediately, the little rebel in me decides that since I am the first one here, I can select a different bed than the one appointed to me. But when the others arrive, the woman whose bed I intended to claim, wants it for herself, and so I retreat to my assigned cot.

One of the other women – a beautiful, dynamic black attorney from Florida named Sandra – says, "You know, I've never done anything like this before, and I'm not sure I can even do it. But I've decided to just follow all the rules and do exactly what they tell me to do." I take her message to heart as a reminder. Hadn't I decided to follow Stephan's directions all these years? I tell Sandra that I was just ordained and am preparing for my first Mass. She's excited for me, and though we don't speak during the ten days, a bond between us is created in those first hours before silence is imposed. The beauty of divine surrender is reiterated to me when I realize that everything that's been given to me, especially the assigned bed, is exactly perfect. (My bed is closest to the bathroom, and my colitis still has me getting up two or three times a night.)

Stephan likes to tease people about retreats, saying, "I never retreat, I always advance." Far from being a retreat, however, this meditation training *is* an advance into the interior world of mind. We sit in the meditation hall for about ten hours a day, with breaks. In the evenings, a dharma talk by Goenka, which had been recorded ten years earlier, is presented. I'm astounded at how relevant each evening's talk is to the deeply interior and personal experience I'm having each day. It's "very scientific," Goenka repeats in his thick Burmese accent.

There are only two meals a day and we are awakened at 4 a.m. The first four days, we focus our attention on only the sensations around the nostrils and upper lip for ten hours each day. By the third day, my mind is quiet and focused, but an awful boredom sets in. *All right already*, my mind complains. But there is nothing other than this attention to be done. As Liv often says, "the only way out is through." I'd decided to follow the instruction, and although there are people who get up and go outside, I only allow myself to leave the meditation hall during the official breaks. I stay with the boredom, and at the moment in which I come to fully accept it, suddenly, like the proverbial sunshine breaking through the clouds, a deep happiness oozes through me. I feel like shouting, *Is everybody happy?* I've found the "pearl of great price"![16] There is no new car or lover, no winning lottery number. This happiness has been inside of me all along. It comes from nothing more than my own being.

After sitting with this attention on the nostrils and the sensations around the upper lip, the course takes us to a more complex practice: we can start paying attention to all the sensations in the body, not just the nostrils. On day eight, anger arises and I observe it. That evening during the dharma talk, the voice of Goenka that had been recorded ten years earlier says, "You might be experiencing some anger today." *How does he know?* "It's very scientific," the Burmese accent echoes in my mind.

I find the silence liberating. It takes a lot of energy simply to be polite: Hello, how are you today? with a smile designed to conceal what is inside and not to offend. In the *Gospel of Thomas*, Jesus says, "Do not lie and do not do what you hate." I spent many weeks contemplating the depth and breadth of the meaning of that passage. If just saying "I'm fine" in answer to "how are you today?" is a lie covering up how you really are, how many more lies do we tell ourselves consciously and unconsciously round the clock, day in and day out?

I wear the clothes I designed, long loose dresses, which easily accommodate cross-legged sitting. One of my garments, a rayon ruana (a shawl-like wrap) is perfect for the meditation hall. I drape it over my shoulders when the air conditioner comes on, or

---

[16] "The 'Pearl' is the Living Gnosis, or again, the self-realization of the Logos in man..."
*Echoes From the Gnosis*, Vol. X, by G.R.S. Mead.

slip it off when the room grows warm, without much movement or perturbation.

We are allowed to walk about the paths and around the pond during the breaks. Free from concerns for social interaction, while walking I become very attentive to my posture, pace, and rhythm.

On the final day when we are allowed to talk, a group of women from various cabins congregate in the dorm in which I've stayed. We all exude the happiness I'd discovered that fourth day. Sitting on the cots, we laugh and share our experiences, thoughts, insights, and observations. The energy in the room is turbulent with a joyous cloud of survival stories: *"We did it!" "I almost left, but the teacher talked me into staying, and I'm so happy I did." "You look so much younger than when you first arrived."* Everyone has a particular voice bouncing through her mind, freely, like a red rubber ball in an empty room – the loving voice of Goenka with his thick Burmese accent. One woman turns to me and says, "Every time I saw you in the distance I thought you looked like Jesus – your clothes, and the way you walk." Sandra and I look at each other and laugh. "She is," Sandra says. "She is Jesus." And we laugh again.

One of the commitments during the course is to set aside rituals, prayers, and all other forms of worship just for the ten days. "Give the practice a fair trial," Goenka says. "Make it an experiment." By the end of the course I recognize, *We don't have anything like this in the Gnostic practice.* We have rituals and prayers and myths, but we don't have any singular meditation technique that guides people, step by step, to the interior mind – a way not just to acknowledge discord, to pray for redemption, but to actively dissolve discord and generate redemption. The Buddha said, "You have to work out your own liberation."

I contemplated the thought of bringing something like this to the church, knowing "Da Boss" would never accept other practices into his Ecclesia. John Goelz was also very active in a Buddhist sangha, but he never mixed his two religions. Stephan spent his life resurrecting what he understood to be a pure Gnostic expression, and he didn't want it to become, as he put it, "tapioca pudding."

# CHAPTER 11

# First Mass of a New Priest

Stephan had a flyer printed up in red to announce my first Mass:

YOU ARE INVITED TO THE FESTIVAL
OF THE HOLY MARY MAGDALENE
Sunday, July 26, 1998, AT 11 A.M.
The first Mass of a new priest is an occasion for special graces; please come and welcome our new priest to her new office.

I'd practiced saying Mass so often at the private chapel with Stephan and Michael, amending little things here and there per Stephan's critiques, that by the time of my first public Mass in the main church, I felt confident and at ease with my performance. I wore the antique Catholic chasuble that Lance had given me as an ordination gift, and felt calm and full of love and generosity. There was an atmosphere of pomp, and the small storefront church was filled. It was a hot summer day, made more stifling for the clergy by our extra members positioned around the altar, as well as the layers of polyester and silk vestments.

Michael stands behind me to my left as crosier bearer. About ten minutes into the ceremony, as I am about to begin reading the Gospel, something indefinable alerts me to turn to my left, and I see Michael about to faint – his eyelids are half closed and he is leaning slightly. I step over to him, take the crosier, hand it to Jack-the-Bear to place in the stand, and help Michael step behind the curtain to sit down on a bench. All the other clergy remain at their posts not moving, as if this were part of the choreography. I get Michael a glass of water and speak to him long enough to be assured he's OK, then glide back to my place at the altar and proceed. I have never known myself to possess this degree of composure. A deep calm has settled in me, which has heretofore not yet manifested. I feel finally in possession of a dignity that has always been at the center of my being, yet taken years to come to expression. My twin spirit is now standing inside of me.

∞

Homilies are given at the end of the Mass, and Stephan has the great capacity to both give a homily extemporaneously, and to make everyone present feel that he is speaking to them personally. That is the goal and intent of a homily, but for my first time delivering one, I've written it out. I've printed out little booklets of my talk, covered in turquoise card stock and tied with red yarn – the pair of colors I fell in love with on the day that Jan revealed their relationship, when he took my brush and painted a thin halo of turquoise around my burning red chalice. The juxtaposition of these two colors speaks to me of spirit because of the way they had ignited my chalice painting that day. Before the Mass, I place one booklet on each chair, as a gift to the congregants.

I begin my homily with a quote from Thoreau about walking. This is a section of Thoreau's writing that Roger begins his two-year course with: "If you have paid your debts, and made your will, and settled all your affairs, and are a free man – then you are ready for a walk." I relate Thoreau's concept of taking a walk to living in the divine ocean of surrender without attachments.

As this is Mary Magdalene's Feast Day, I framed my homily around her. I speak of the wild love Mary Magdalene shared with Jesus. The Gnostic scriptures say that Mary Magdalene was Jesus's consort. Why did they refer to her as his consort? I suggest that it was no metaphor but simple truth. She was his wife and spiritual companion.

*Why was she labeled a prostitute, an adulteress? I have a theory that the ones who named her thus were prostituting their own souls to the princes of power and adulterating the true mystery. It was, on a grand historical scale, simple projection of their disowned collective shadow.*

*The other apostles asked, "Why do you love her more than all of us?" Jesus answered, "Why do I not love you like her?" (Don't Jews always answer a question with a question?)*

*Why did he love her more than the rest? Have you ever loved another for her otherness? Have you ever loved wherein you experience a movement and a rest? Where communion with another nurtures space between for "The Friend," for God to be present?*

*If you have ever loved in this way, then you know why Jesus loved Mary Magdalene more than all the rest. She participated in the mystery of Jesus himself. While the others were asking questions like "Should we circumcise? Should we keep kosher? What new rules should we abide by? (To paraphrase The Gospel of Thomas), Mary Magdalene was shamelessly breaking all protocol. She burst into a house of men and with tears and hair flowing, "wasting" precious oils, she demonstrated her abandonment to Love. Like many mystics, those who have been dissolved by love, she baffled and probably frightened the corralled and curtailed minds of the men surrounding her. But Jesus knew her passion and shared his passion with her. Thus she was his most accurate witness. Mary Magdalene reveals the deepest of the feminine mysteries. She is the cornerstone the builders rejected.[17] Her passion tore at the boundaries. That is why Jesus loved her more than the others. She was willing, as Thoreau prescribed, to take a walk.*

*May we, too, in due course, learn to walk toward the unknown with eyes and heart open to whatever "thou dost appoint." And may the mystery of that which hangs 'twixt Heaven and Earth descend upon us and remain with us always. Amen."*

---

[17] Jesus said, "Show me the stone that the builders rejected: that is the keystone."
The Gospel of Thomas, logion 66. (Logia are sayings or maxims attributed to Christ but of which there is no written record or mention in the Gospels.)

The homily ends, and the custom is that the new priest then gives an extra blessing to the congregants who wish it. The kneeler is brought forward, and everyone in the congregation comes up to be blessed. Blessedness moves through me. I have given myself over to this love and have become a vessel for it. The mood in the little storefront church this afternoon is exultant. Bobbie comes up to me afterward with a smile as wide as the sky, her robin's egg eyes radiant with joy. Joy – that's what permeates the room: the same joy I felt erupt in me during those days of silent meditation.

# Splitting Horses — Find Me There

In my fifth year of Roger Weir's two-year educational yoga, which he presented continually year after year, I was moving deeper into the saturation of wisdom. Though Roger was very knowledgeable about Gnosticism, what he taught was not limited to any system, religion, doctrine, or mythos. His teaching was differential, not mythological, and the true voice within me that was ever my guide was certain about my commitment to his offering. Something began to occur in my soul. The two horses that I'd been riding for five years – Roger Weir's education and Stephan's ritual practices – were beginning to veer in distinctly separate trajectories. I felt a decision moving progressively toward me that I would have to meet.

∞

My father once told me "You know, you never spent months holding onto tables and knees learning how to walk. You crawled for a couple of months, and then one day you just stood up and walked across the room."

"I remember learning how to ride a two-wheeler like that, too," I said. I was visiting my parents, and we were sitting around the long wooden dining-room table reminiscing.

"Yeah," my mother scowled. "I looked out the window and saw you sailing off down the street with the other kids in the neighborhood, and it scared me to death. It was only the day before that you needed Dad to balance you with the training wheels on."

"It's just that when I get something, I get it whole, as if I've always known it," I said.

∞

In March of 1999, I said my first-year-anniversary Mass. Like a pot of water coming to boil, my soul was beginning to feel the kind of perturbation that eventually causes a sea change. I'd been reading *And There Was Light*, the autobiography of Jacques Lusseyran, who was known as the blind hero of the French Resistance. His writing was not related to the lexicon of Gnostic tractates, and veering from church custom, I quoted heavily from his book in my homily:

"I was aware of a radiance emanating from a place I knew nothing about, a place which might as well have been outside me as within. But radiance was there, or, to put it more precisely, light. I found light and joy at the same moment, and I can say without hesitation that from that time on, light and joy have never been separated in my experience."

Lusseyran had been blinded as a child and discovered that he could actually see by means of this light. He was speaking of it literally, whereas the Gnostic material used light as a metaphor. I was coming to recognize that the most mysterious qualities of spirituality are not imagined, mythical, or metaphorical, but actual. Religious ritual context is a phase of conscious development, but there are mysteries that extend far beyond myth and ritual. As Goenka insisted in his Vipassana trainings, the other shore – the Buddha's state of being "awake" – is attained "scientifically" and not mythically. One cannot reach that state of awakening by rituals or ceremonies or hope.

My homily concluded as a personal confession:

*Being a priest for me is a verb not a noun. For one year, I have wondered, What does this verb do? Where does it find its references if not in static identifiable qualities? This has become a field of inquiry for me with no ready-made answers, no thing to point to – no label (or collar) to identify myself as. I don't in any way claim to have achieved anything whatsoever. All that I have done is respond to the will of an impulse that is very real inside of my being.*

∞

Stephan had been patient, waiting for me to make my trip to Cotters to buy the one item that would complete my vestment ensemble – a collar. Though I'd seen other clergy rush off to buy a collar as soon as they were ordained to the deaconate, I was not compelled to make that purchase. Initially, when I was a deacon, the collar was simply not a focus of my concern, but as time went on it began to carry symbolic overtones. A collar was the signifying identity of a priest. "People treat me differently when I wear a collar," Michael said. "I have little Hispanic mothers coming up to me in the hospital asking me to pray for their son." I had no desire to become the symbolic *idea* of a priest. I felt the *nature* of my priesthood too deeply.

I remain in my practice with the Gnostic church. Sometimes I say Mass in the main church, sometimes in the private chapel with Stephan and Michael, but mostly in the role of deacon or subdeacon, because Stephan is usually the celebrant. One Sunday I am standing as subdeacon and facing the end of the altar. My hands are together in prayer position and I am chanting the Canticle, the Kyrie, bowing, kneeling, and reading the lesson. As suddenly as when I walked across the room from crawling when I was nine months old; and when I took off on my two-wheeler without training wheels, the voice of wisdom speaks very clearly within me: *Your time with the Gnostic church is completed; if you stay you will become angry, sick, and disruptive. It is time to move on.*

∞

"You've extended yourself so deeply," Stephan said, as we sat in his apartment surrounded by rare esoteric trinkets and ritual implements, drinking strong Turkish coffee from porcelain demitasses. "There's no need to make such a severe decision. Why don't you take some time off? It is not unusual for a priest to feel overload from time to time." But it wasn't overload that I felt. The VIII of Cups Tarot image hovered in my consciousness, where a man is walking off into the hills, leaving his row of cups behind. "If you see my back, Stephan, it is because I am moving forward, deeper into the mystery that resides in my being." Isn't that what "gnosis" is? I was not walking away or retreating. I'd known from the beginning that church ritual was only at the surface of my experience. I was not walking away from my responsibility to the "Light;" it *was* the "Light" that called me onward.

∞

Stephan had been deeply disappointed by most of the women he'd ordained or consecrated: The Frenchwoman whose heritage was Languedoc – the language and region of latter-day Gnostics known as Cathars; the daughter of a Gnostic priest; and others. He had so wanted to contain their feminine essence at the center of his circle. But he was unable to allow the feminine her wilderness and unpredictable passions. I doubt he would have appreciated an ardent red-haired beauty storming into his Mass and falling to her knees to anoint his feet. As Stephan admitted, he always advanced, never retreated. But the feminine energies go not just higher and forward, but also deeper, back to the deepest of mysteries, deepest of feelings, the depths of the unconscious, as I had done as a very young child, crying on the lawn with eternal sorrow. I brought that depth with me, and ironically it was Stephan's masculine form of initiation that was able to provide a channel for its development. However, like a birth canal that provides passage for the infant to come into being, if she were to stay in that passage, both she and her mother would die.

I felt an affinity with Mary Magdalene, the feminine aspect, the other side of the mystery; Magdalene's true partnership is with the living Christ. Not the symbol nor the idea, not the rituals nor mythologies, but the ever-changing, ever-renewing, un-corral-able *Living Word*.

# CHAPTER 12

# After

For seven years, I had devoted myself to the ritual process, inching my way through what felt like a long birth canal – dark and uncertain, where the only way out was through. Each sacramental phase was like a contraction, advancing me toward the unknown. I had faithfully followed my inner voice, which urged me to keep going onward. That voice was truer than any other, and so I kept going. With my ordination to the priesthood, that long dark corridor was no more, and I felt I'd been birthed out onto an open field. I'd served as a priest within the church context for almost two years.

Several months after leaving the church I sat on a green plastic Adirondack chair under the huge pepper tree in our backyard in Topanga and asked the inner voice of wisdom that had admonished me to leave the church, *What am I supposed to do now?* I still had no desire to put on an identity, just as I had resisted putting on the collar. I waited for the answer to come to me, but no answer came. I scanned the themes of my life: wild love, freedom, "living by the light of Jesus." Then it dawned on me that I was asking the wrong question. My initiation to the priesthood had restored my soul to a wholeness that had been lost at a very young age. I now possessed a degree of "free will," for I had been drawn through the veil of sorrow that had pulled me under, crying on the lawn when I was a child. Intention that is born from a cloudy mind, a damaged soul full of miscomprehension and delusion is not actually "free will" but just a chain of causation. I'd become "person" enough to ask the right questions, and I realized that the right question now was, *"What do I want to do?"* In the *Gospel of Thomas*, the disciples ask Jesus what the new laws are. They are asking, what are the limits, the confines, the rules? Jesus replies, "Don't lie and don't do what you hate."

Hillel, the great Jewish sage and scholar, from 100 B.C., asked, "If I am not for myself, who will be for me, and if I am only for myself what am I?" My initiation brought me to an interior priest-hood where knowing what I want inherently includes what is best for all. I'd come to a place of knowing that if I am not for the good of the whole, my personal desires are worthless. The question "What do I want?" is new with every asking; Jesus did say, "Behold, I make all things new." This is freedom, this is wild love, this is *living close by the light of Jesus Christ.*

# Perfection

My initiation with Stephan and his particular Gnostic liturgy was preparation for my furthering on *The Way*.

I began writing this memoir from a phrase that appeared in my mind one morning, nine years ago: *Love on the Brink of History.*

I thought, *that sounds like the title of a book.*

The inner voice said, *It is the book you are to write.*

I asked, *what is it about?*

The inner voice said, *write it and find out.*

For the past nine years I've worked and scrapped, and rewritten. I've loved and hated, been bored with and inspired by what you have just read, struggling to understand what "love on the brink of history" means. There is a historical tsunami wave upon us now, where love is crashing against the shores of fundamentalist mental forms, of saber rattling, of ever more thrilling sense experiences, of sordid scandals, and greed beyond reason. I continue to listen toward *The Way*. I continue to listen toward deep wisdom, submitting to what needs to be done.

$$\infty$$

Just as I finished this final draft I received a gift from my mother as I had received my true name from my father.

While celebrating her 90th birthday, my family sits casually around the dining-room table asking questions about the past and reminiscing. The village where I was born in Israel is named Beit Herut. My mother says, "Beit Herut. That means House of Freedom."

*What immortal hand or eye does frame this perfect symmetry.*

# Resources

Roger Weir: www.sharedpresencefoundation.com

Gnosticism: www.gnosis.org

*The Gospel of Thomas* can be found in both gnosis.org and *The Nag Hammadi Library.*

*The Hymn of the Pearl*, also known as *The Hymn of the Robe of Glory* can be found in gnosis.org.

Dreams and Dreamtime: www.mossdreams.com

Vipassana Meditation: www.dhamma.org

*The Nag Hammadi Library*, published by Harper and Row; reissued as *The Nag Hammadi Scriptures* by Harper One

*Hermetica*, edited and translated by Sir Walter Scott, published by Shambhala

*The Other Bible: Ancient Esoteric Texts*, edited by Willis Barnstone, published by Harper Collins.

www.ingramcontent.com/pod-product-compliance
Lightning Source LLC
Chambersburg PA
CBHW022129080426
42734CB00006B/280